It Needs To Be Done

How to persuade others to do it

with less hassle and stress

DICK COCHRAN

Note: The action skills in this book have been adapted from the work of Bob Weyant and used with permission of Bob Weyant and Libby Wagner. For more information, visit www.influencingoptions.com.

The SOCIAL STYLE Model™ is a trademark of The TRACOM Group and SOCIAL STYLE references are used with permission. Visit www.tracomcorp.com for more information.

Special Thanks to:

Barbara McNichol for editing the content to make much better sense out what I thought was perfectly clear. And for creatively adding better ways to express my ideas. Great job. Contact her at www.BarbaraMcNichol.com

Dee Dukehart "super proofer" for finding and correcting punctuation I didn't even know existed. Contact her at www.DeeDukehart.com

© 2015 by COMStar
3375A West 111th Loop
Westminster, CO 80031
Phone (303) 666-4224
www.comstar.us

TABLE OF CONTENTS

INTRODUCTION
Where did this handbook come from? 1
NERDS NEED PEOPLE SKILLS
How will this handbook help? 2
THE HISTORY
How is this handbook organized? 4
DYNAMIC INFLUENCING MODEL
What's the big picture of how to influence people? 7
INFLUENCING PROCESS
How do I get people to change their behavior? 8
SIX ACTION SKILLS
What skills do I need to influence others? 12
ADAPTATION SKILLS
With Whom do I need to build rapport? 15
How do I communicate with people who are different? 16
DETERMINE THE REAL ISSUE
How do I get people to focus on the Real Issue? 46
BUILD THE TRUST
How do I get people to better work with me? 72
PERSUASION SKILLS
How do I persuade people to do what needs to be done? ... 85
CONFRONT WITHOUT CONFLICT
How do I keep from creating conflict? 86
CLARIFY THE RESPONSE
Am I getting a clear "yes" or a clear "no"? 104
GIVE POSITIVE FEEDBACK
How do I make "yes" easier in future interactions? 120
MAKING IT ALL WORK
Okay, what do I do next? 127
COMMIT TO GROWING
When will I get good? 128
DOCUMENT YOUR SUCCESS
How do I master the concepts? 130
LEARN BY TEACHING
Who do I interact with to master the concepts? 132
MAKE A BEHAVIOR CONTRACT
How do I stay committed? 134
Meet the Author 136

Questions and Answers

When we have a communication problem; we can quickly identify the question but often have no idea where to find the answer. This table helps you locate the section of this handbook that will address the frequently asked questions.

Question	Page
➤ How do I get people to change their behavior?	8
➤ Why are people so different?	19
➤ Why don't they understand what I'm saying?	26
➤ How do I get buy in?	29
➤ What do I do when C.R.A.P. happens?	46
➤ Why are some people always whining?	54
➤ How do I insure people will keep their commitments?	60
➤ How do I keep them owning the problem?	62
➤ How do I handle confrontation?	86
➤ What do I do to get the performance I need?	91
➤ How do I handle smoke screens?	111
➤ How do I handle emotional reactions?	114
➤ How do I make "yes" easier in future interactions?	120
➤ When will my changes start getting results?	128

INTRODUCTION

Where did this handbook come from?

How will this handbook help?

The "why" for this handbook is obvious to those of us who have a technical bent and have experienced "difficulties" working with people. Most non-technical people refer to us as "nerds" or "geeks." I believe that the proper term is "technology professional." This broad definition includes anyone with a technical degree or technical background. You've heard people say, "They're nerds: great with technology, but not so good with people."

It's not our fault. We weren't taught People Skills in school. You might think that being in the family would be a good place to learn them. Unfortunately, most of us (non-nerds included) don't come from fully functioning families, so we didn't learn People Skills there, either.

That leaves learning these skills in the workplace, the school of hard knocks. The problem with this "school" is that you never know which lesson is coming next and by the time you "graduate," you might be too old to practice all of those lessons.

This handbook brings together all of the communications skills I've gathered during my 20 years in the electronics industry combined with another 20 years in my training and consulting company. Use it to shortcut your learning curve and increase your effectiveness with others. Most important, you can reduce the stress of those interactions.

I know your frustration. Why should I have to get people to do what they either know they should do or are getting paid to do? Simple answer: "It is what it is." But the good news is that the skills you gain here will help you make it happen.

Not only do the People Skills you'll learn get results in the workplace, they also apply in all of your interactions. Wouldn't it be great to be more effective with the groups you're involved with outside of work? And wouldn't it be especially great to more effectively interact with your co-workers, friends, and loved ones?

How is this handbook organized?

I was educated to become an electrical engineer. After college, I got a well-paying job based on that technical knowledge. Because I performed well on the job, I was given incrementally more responsibility at work. Things were going well . . . until my boss said to me, "Dick, to reward you, we want to make you a manager." I felt pleased and a little nervous as I said, "Great, I'll do it." I hadn't managed people before, but I felt proud to be chosen.

I didn't know it at the time, but that decision would haunt me for years. You see, the people on my team wanted to have a say in what we did. They wanted recognition for their ideas. They didn't always agree with me, their boss. When it came to dealing with my team, my technical skills did not serve me.

One of the worst events in my career happened when the human resources people called me into a conference room so my team could tell me what I was doing wrong. I heard the words "uncaring, aloof, and unsympathetic." I promised to try harder; that was all I knew how to do. Then I went home to my wife Mary Ann, looking for sympathy and support. She was already upset with something I'd done (or not done) and before long was using the words "uncaring, aloof, and unsympathetic." I accused her of talking to my people at work. "No," she said, "but isn't it interesting that we have the same list of complaints": The same list.

That's when the light bulb went on for me. Clearly, I needed more than technical skills to be successful. But where would I learn them? That started a quest to find and adopt People Skills that would work. I took seminars, I read books, I studied at the school of hard knocks, and finally I found a gifted mentor named Bob Weyant, who shared with me a set of People Skills that really worked.

My search for answers transferred into starting my own company, COMStar, to bring the People Skills I learned to technology professionals like me. For 20 years, COMStar has taught these skills in public seminars and as in-house training programs for individual companies.

Over the years, one group of clients has emerged that especially benefits from these skills—project managers. These people are uniquely situated to use the Influencing Skills noted here to bring together a team that produces results on target, on time, and on budget. I've been associated with the Project Management Institute (PMI) and the global professional association of project managers for more than 15 years. The skills in this handbook have been honed through chapter training programs as well as through the PMI SeminarsWorld® program.

These skills will complement your technical skills, improve your results, and reduce your hassles. I've organized and integrated them into the cohesive format you see throughout this handbook.

If Technical Skills Make You Valuable,

Then People Skills Make You Invaluable

Consider this your handbook of solutions to everyday people problems. Used as a reference manual, you have a place to find how-to answers to specific problems, allowing you to get more done through other people. The skills have been proven to work in a variety of situations.

You can also use it as a textbook on how to influence people's behaviors. Reading the handbook in a linear fashion will reveal the relevant skills needed to ensure a high degree of success in getting the right behaviors.

First, be aware that the People Skills in this handbook have a basis in the Social Sciences: Psychology, Sociology, Linguistics, etc. Those who have benefited from it include technology professionals in state and city government organizations. Beneficiaries also come from manufacturing companies, finance departments in research organizations, educational institutions, military organizations, and management teams from technology companies.

Second, the highly structured skills in this handbook are designed to maximize your success in working with others and minimize the chances of conflict. It's a fill-in-the-blank approach that includes the proper words to say. Mastering these skills will keep you from becoming defensive and prevent negative reactions from those with whom you're interacting.

Caution: Don't mess around with the words and structure until you get comfortable with the skills themselves.

With practice, you'll be able to adapt these skills "on the fly" to new situations, and each new skill will feel more natural.

You may already be familiar with some of the tools in this handbook, but not how they are used in real-life situations. Other tools will be new and are worth trying out. Definitely expect one or two tools to have a major, positive impact on your interactions with others. In particular, look for those tools that can make a tremendous difference to your sense of wellbeing.

At a minimum, applying these new People Skills won't make the situation worse than normal. Be brave: Try them with diligence, and your results will improve.

DYNAMIC INFLUENCING MODEL

What's the big picture of how to influence people?

How do I get people to change their behavior?

This handbook is about the Influencing Process to change behaviors—a person's performance, actions, and demeanor that are observable, even measurable. It's not about changing a person's attitudes, beliefs, mindset, or philosophy—what's hidden in a person's mind.

Behavior versus Attitude:

I can't make someone respect me in the workplace (an attitude). I can't see into the mind to know if and when it changes. It's hidden from me. But I can ask for respectful behavior: e.g., Say hello when we meet in the hall, don't interrupt me in a meeting, and don't call me a "dummy." I can observe whether or not I am getting those behaviors.

If you focus on changing people's behaviors,

sometimes a change in their attitudes will follow.

The Dynamic Influencing Process is about getting others to do something that needs to be done—to take action. Maybe it relates to a specific task or a shift in behavior. Because they haven't seen the need to take action on their own, they often have to be persuaded, which is sometimes easy and sometimes difficult.

What follows is a flow chart that shows all the elements involved to successfully influence another person. Start at the upper left with a need for the other person to do something. What is the specific action or change in behavior you want to see? It is critical to know what you want so you can recognize when you get it.

8

Let's assume you determined what needs to be done.

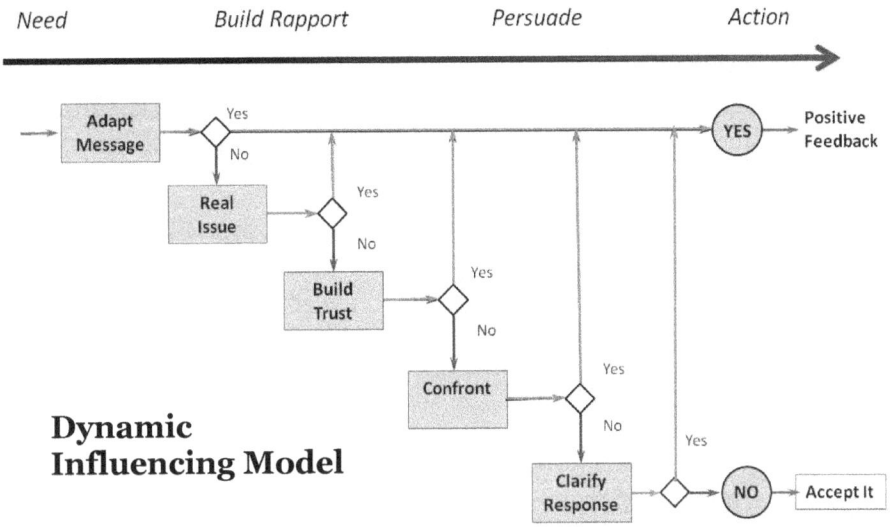

Need   Build Rapport   Persuade   Action

Dynamic Influencing Model

Adapt Message → Yes → Positive Feedback / No → Real Issue → Yes / No → Build Trust → Yes / No → Confront → Yes / No → Clarify Response → Yes → NO → Accept It / Yes

Simply understanding the top line alone will help you more effectively get action to happen. On the left is the need to do something. First, make sure you have established rapport to make them comfortable working with you. Then persuade them to take the action. They say "yes," and the desired action happens.

Let's look at this Action Flow Chart in more detail. The first step is to adapt the message to make sure the other person hears and understands your request.

As you know, communication is not automatic between people. In fact, as you'll see later in this handbook, people fall into four basic SOCIAL STYLES—Amiable, Analytical, Driving, Expressive. Unfortunately, these social styles do not easily communicate with each other; built into them is misunderstanding and even conflict. That creates a need to adapt the message to the other person's communication style as a way to make sure what you're asking is heard.

So you adapted the request for a change in behavior and asked for action. If you get a "yes," that's great. After the action is complete, then provide positive feedback as reinforcement. But, what if you don't get that "yes"? Sometimes people can't say "yes" because they're not sure you're addressing the real issue or they don't believe anyone knows the actual problem at this point. How many times have you focused on one thing only to find the real problem lurking in the background?

The task then becomes determining what the real issue is. Once you've done that, reconstruct your request around it, ask again, and when you get a "yes," you're home free.

Another lurking issue might prevent people from saying "yes": They don't trust you. As a premise of this Influencing Process, having high trust already means you're likely to get a "yes" to your request. If the trust is low, then it's important to build trust and maintain it at a level that eventually earns the "yes" to your request.

These first three areas—adapt the message, determine what's the real issue, and build trust—have skills associated with them called Adaptation Skills. These skills are used to build rapport with another person and open a clear pathway to communications.

But establishing rapport may not be enough. Suppose you have adapted the message, determined the real issue, and built the trust. You still have to persuade the person to take action. You may have to confront the person to change a "no" to a "yes," coming face to face with him or her without causing conflict or defensiveness. You would make a request for behavior change in a way that shows the other person the positive consequences of saying "yes." If this confrontation step works, great, you have your "yes."

If not, what sometimes happens? The person doesn't give a clear "yes" or "no" answer, so you have to clarify the response in order to take action. Once you do, you use strategies to handle the response—either to get the "yes" nailed down or to change the "no" into a "yes."

Once you get a "yes" and the action happens, then you get "insurance" to make it easier the next time. How? By giving positive feedback to those involved. This also falls into the Persuasion Skills group because positive feedback, given correctly, increases your chances of getting a "yes" the next time you have to ask.

These Persuasion Skills—confront without conflict, clarify the response, give positive feedback—help others realize the benefits of saying "yes" to your request.

No is okay. Notice the "NO" on the flow chart in the lower right corner. The truth is people can rarely be made to do something, especially in the workplace. And they always have the right to say "no."

Consider two cases. One case is saying "no" and giving a valid business reason while staying open to negotiation. For example, "No, I can't help you now because I have six things on my plate that my boss just gave me. If I didn't have them, I'd be glad to help."

Case two is saying "no" and being willing to live with the consequences. That means you aren't trying to persuade people to do something against their will. Rather, you present both the positive and negative consequences in such a way that people choose to do the requested behavior.

I know this flow chart might look a little overwhelming, but it pictures the whole process. No doubt, you are already using some form of these skills. From now on, when you run into communication difficulties, you have a model for troubleshooting the situation. You can also use this model to focus on where you need to expand your skill set.

I encourage you to use this handbook to learn specific skills in various areas. When you do, you'll see increased success come your way.

What skills do I need to influence others?

To recap, the six Action Skills needed in the Influencing Process are grouped into two categories: Adaptation Skills and Persuasion Skills, as noted in the previous flow chart.

The Adaptation Skills are used to build rapport with others, create an environment of high trust, and adapt your message to their SOCIAL STYLE. Your goal is to remove barriers to effective communication so the person you're communicating with can hear and understand what you're asking.

The Persuasion Skills are used to help the other person understand the benefits and positive consequences of choosing the behavior you're asking for. They give you options and different approaches to turn a "no" into a "yes." They also give you confidence that you can be in control of the interaction even when things get difficult.

Let's examine these six skills.

Adaptation Skills

These three Adaptation Skills establish rapport and set up an environment for successful communication. In these brief descriptions, you'll see what you'll learn going forward as you apply the lessons in this handbook.

1.) Adapt the Message. Each of us has a unique style of communicating, with styles falling into four general categories. After defining the model, we show you how to determine your style and quickly identify the other person's style. Then we explain where some of the built-in miscommunication comes from and how to overcome it.

2.) Determine the Real Issue. Being able to identify the real issue is important in handling unexpected problems. Do you spend too much time whining, moaning, and groaning about a problem instead of solving it? We show you a Problem-Solving Process and provide the tools to help you and others move through it effectively. We also provide tools that help ensure the expected actions take place.

3.) Build Trust. Creating a high trust environment is essential to maximize the performance of teams and groups. In fact, trust is a critical factor in all of our interactions. We identify the Core Dimensions that build trust, show how to preserve it, and identify unintentional ways we destroy the trust we have.

Persuasion Skills

Why do we need Persuasion Skills? Because most people are perfectly content to keep doing what they are already doing. And if they're looking to do something different, it's probably not what you need them to do.

We address three areas to help you persuade people to recognize the benefits of doing what you request.

4.) Confront Without Conflict. Most people experience that confrontation often results in conflict. We provide a new definition of conflict and show how to confront someone without creating conflict. We also provide tools to help you be more in control of a situation and generate a successful outcome.

5.) Clarify the Response. Much of the time, people don't respond to a request with a clear "yes" or "no" answer. How can you clarify their response and deal with it using strategies for changing a "no" into a "yes"? We address this and provide skills to deal with the emotional responses that often make you feel uncomfortable.

6.) Give Positive Feedback. This is a powerful, long-term Persuasion Skill few people use effectively. Giving positive feedback boosts the probability the next request will be a "yes." We show you how to make the feedback you give more effective.

Accept the "No"

To reiterate: people always have the right to say "no" to a request, which is okay when they give a valid business reason and stay open to negotiation. A "no" response is also okay if the other person is willing to live with the consequences that will follow.

Remember, you can't make people do something. Rather, you can only spell out the consequences of their action—both positive and negative.

ADAPTATION
SKILLS

With whom do I need to build rapport?

How do I communicate with people who are different?

Communication between people is not automatic. With some people, we hit it off and can easily talk with them: We "click." With others, we find an almost instant barrier. Something in their SOCIAL STYLE puts us off: We "clunk."

Differences in social styles were the subject of a breakthrough study by Dr. David Merrill and the resulting model he created called the SOCIAL STYLE Model™.

Know the SOCIAL STYLE Model

Dr. Merrill found that, over time, we are consistent in our basic approach to communicating with others. SOCIAL STYLE represents the most persistent, socially evident pattern of behavior that a person demonstrates to others. When we can understand the pattern, we can communicate better and even better predict behavior in certain circumstances.

Assertiveness

The first thing we notice about people is their assertiveness. Do they walk right up and introduce themselves or do they hang back and wait to be approached?

At one end of the Assertiveness spectrum are the "Tellers" who state their opinions with assurance. They make positive statements and declarations. They say what they think and feel, and often they tell you what you should think, feel, and do. They are more "in your face" than other styles.

At the other end of the spectrum are the "Askers" who are more cautious in sharing their opinions. They ask what you think and feel in a quiet way. They attempt to influence through asking rather than telling.

Here are typical Assertiveness behaviors: things people say and do:

Ask Behaviors:

- Speaks slowly

- Talks little

- Talks quietly

- Pauses a lot

- Waits to speak

- Leans back

- Indirect eye contact

- Points infrequently

- Acts carefully

- Cooperates

Tell Behaviors:

- Speaks rapidly

- Talks a lot

- Talks loudly

- Takes few pauses

- Interrupts others

- Leans forward

- Strong eye contact

- Points a lot

- Takes risks

- Competes

Where would you put yourself on this horizontal Assertiveness axis?

Responsiveness

The second most noticeable aspect of behavior Dr. Merrill identified is the level of a person's Responsiveness. Responsiveness measures how much feeling people show. Some tightly control their display of feelings, not letting them out much, so it's hard to "read" them. They're called "Poker Faced."

On the other end of the Responsiveness spectrum are the "Emoters" who let their feelings show all the time. Whenever they are either happy or sad, it's heard in their voice and seen in their faces and body language.

Here are typical Responsiveness behaviors: things people say and do:

Control Behaviors:

- Prefers facts and data

- Is task-oriented

- Less voice inflection

- Values logic, thinking

- Tells opinions, stories

- Is people-oriented

- More voice inflection

- Values feelings

- Uses little expression

- Has rigid posture

- Acts aloof with people

- Listen to information

- Uses facial animation

- Has casual posture

- Connects with people

- Listens for relationships

Emote Behaviors:

Where would you put yourself on this vertical Responsiveness axis?

FOUR SOCIAL STYLES

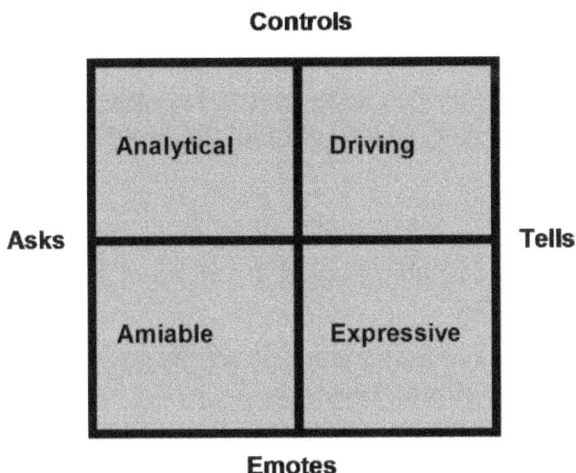

Controls

Analytical	Driving
Amiable	Expressive

Asks   **Tells**

Emotes

The two dimensions—Assertiveness (Ask vs. Tell) and Responsiveness (Control vs. Emote)—define four different SOCIAL STYLES. The quadrants shown here are descriptions of behaviors, not a judgment—that is, being dominant in one quadrant is no better than another.

In general, 25% of the population is in each quadrant. Highly effective people are found in all four quadrants, including presidents, successful coaches, and great movie stars.

In fact, this model holds true for most countries and cultures in the world. The difference lies in what behaviors represent the midpoint on the axis. For example, people from one culture may have a higher average assertiveness than those from another culture.

Because you're made up of a unique combination of Assertiveness and Responsiveness, your "home-base" SOCIAL STYLE is found somewhere on the matrix. Look at the descriptions for these four quadrants to understand the behaviors of each one. This will help you "read" a person's style and also help identify your "home base." As you read these descriptions, for each one, think of people you know who fit the description. Then ask, "Would I want a person of that style on my team?"

Understand Others' Styles

Driving

The Driving Style describes task-oriented people who are assertive in their behaviors and control the emotions they display.

Want	They want to be in control of situations because they are task and results oriented. It's all about getting things done now.
Focus	Their focus is, therefore, on setting goals and accomplishing tasks.
Time	Their time frame is now. They don't want to waste time, and they get irritated when someone fritters away their time. They tend to think they own time. Others had better not be late, but it's okay for them to be late, especially if they are finishing a task.
Work Style	They like to work fast and don't mind working alone if it finishes the task sooner.
Appear	Because of their task focus and controlling their emotions and thoughts, they appear aloof and demanding.
Avoid	Because of their need to accomplish tasks, they are action oriented. They believe if they don't act, the task won't get done. They really avoid inactivity and become impatient with delays.
Blind Side	They don't see value in spending the time necessary to develop relationships. They rarely put energy into managing feelings while they accomplish their tasks.

These people believe that getting the right tasks on the list and accomplishing them in a timely fashion gets the best business results.

Expressive

Expressive Style people are enthusiastically focused on a future "big picture." They like others to get excited and involved in pursuing their personal vision.

Want	They want to create a vision and "sell" it to others. They like to get others participating in having the fun of being involved and getting work done.
Focus	They focus on their current dreams and ideas. This focus can shift easily to a new, different and more exciting vision.
Time	They dwell on the future—what it will feel and be like when their vision is achieved.
Work Style	They love working with people. They make decisions quickly based on how they feel at the moment. They can easily get excited about a new vision.
Appear	They are enthusiastic, stimulating people. They can also appear flighty and not detail-oriented.
Avoid	They dislike isolation and routine.
Blind Side	They can get so focused on the "big picture" that they don't bother with specifics. They prefer the others involved take care of all details.

They believe that if you have the right, clear "big picture," everyone will be motivated to achieve that vision, and the business will get the best results.

Amiable

Amiable Style people are relationship-oriented. They know if they establish the right relationships, they can accomplish any task. They devote the time necessary to build relationships.

Want	They want to build solid relationships and create a positive human environment to support getting things done.
Focus	Their focus is creating relationships to facilitate getting the work done. The essence of forming good relationships is paying attention to people's motives, feelings, and the interactions between people.
Time	Their time frame is the current environment, and they take the time needed to get to know people and build lasting relationships.
Work Style	They are great team players. They provide the oil to make groups work effectively. They make sure people's feelings are considered along with the facts.
Appear	They appear friendly and concerned. Sometimes they appear to work slowly because they like to maintain a stable environment that fosters good relationships.
Avoid	They avoid conflicts, that can damage relationships.
Blind Side	They can sometimes hesitate to confront situations that may be emotional because of their concern for relationships. This delay can be a detriment to getting tasks accomplished and objectives met.

They believe that building a highly functioning team is the best way to get business results.

Analytical

Analytical Style people like to use data, logic, and reason to build consistent solutions to life's problems and opportunities.

Want	They want an organized, detailed solution that makes sense—one that's based on facts, not feelings. For them, data and logic are keys to getting work done.
Focus	Their focus is on quality processes that can function regardless of the personalities and feelings involved.
Time (size)	Their time frame is historical because they have to go back and look at all the ways that did and didn't work. They want to be sure they are doing it right this time.
Work Style	They work slowly and carefully. They don't mind working alone because they want to get the facts for themselves and take the time to organize their thoughts.
Appear	They appear to others to be distant, slow, and hesitant to take a stand.
Avoid	They tend to avoid personal involvement because of the unpredictability of people. They shy away from group and team-building activities.
Blind Side	The problem for them is understanding that at least half of the population makes their decisions based on feelings. Because the Analytical Style doesn't consider feelings a source of information, they don't include that point of view in their solutions.

They believe the way to get the best business results is to develop the right processes that function independently of the people involved.

Observe SOCIAL STYLE

Home Base

Each of us has the elements of each SOCIAL STYLE to a greater or lesser extent. How can we determine a person's "home base" on the matrix?

The trait noticed first, a person's Assertiveness, is the horizontal axis on the matrix. We all fall somewhere along that line.

In my case, I am fairly assertive (as many people tell me), so my style falls on a vertical line to the right of center.

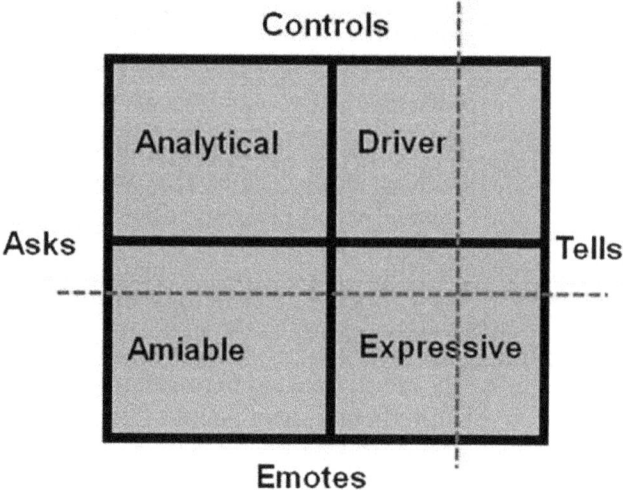

Next, when it comes to controlling

Controls

Analytical	Driver
Amiable	Expressive

Asks   **Tells**

Emotes

versus showing my emotions, my style is on a line below the center line. That means I'm more likely to express emotions than contain them.

Where the two lines intersect is my home base. Someone else's style might intersect in the upper left corner or elsewhere. This matrix shows we can fall in different places on the horizontal and vertical axes.

Where is your home base?

Let me give you more information that may help.

Blended Style

Some people realize they have the characteristics of more than one style; therefore, one descriptor isn't enough.

From my matrix, you see that my home base is in the Expressive quadrant, and my style is close to the Driving quadrant. That

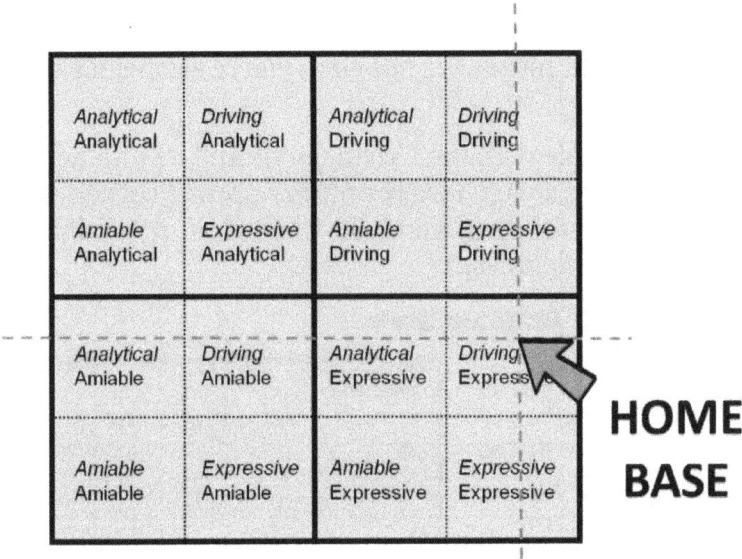

Analytical Analytical	Driving Analytical	Analytical Driving	Driving Driving
Amiable Analytical	Expressive Analytical	Amiable Driving	Expressive Driving
Analytical Amiable	Driving Amiable	Analytical Expressive	Driving Express
Amiable Amiable	Expressive Amiable	Amiable Expressive	Expressive Expressive

HOME BASE

means I have some Driving Style traits in addition to Expressive Style characteristics. When I divide each quadrant into four sub-quadrants and use two adjectives to describe my home base, it becomes Driving-Expressive.

Given that 75 percent of the people you interact with have a social style that differs from yours, it's important to knowing your "home base." It indicates a potential for communication difficulties.

Let's look at some possibilities.

Avoid Communication Difficulties

Cross-Style Conflict

The beauty of this model is that it explains what we have all known all our life: We just can't easily communicate with some people, and it's not anyone's fault.

This happens because two people can be far apart on the SOCIAL STYLE matrix. That means it's not what you're saying, it's the way you're saying it.

Let's take an example with the Driving Style and its interactions with the other three styles. Two people in opposite corners of our matrix are the farthest apart and have the highest potential for communication difficulties.

Driving Style with Amiable Style

Here, the Tell Assertive and highly controlled Driving Style people are so task focused that they don't want to waste time hearing about another's personal life or pets or kids. The Amiable Style people are more Ask Assertive than those with a Driving Style. They want to get to know you and establish a relationship they can count on. They do not want a cool

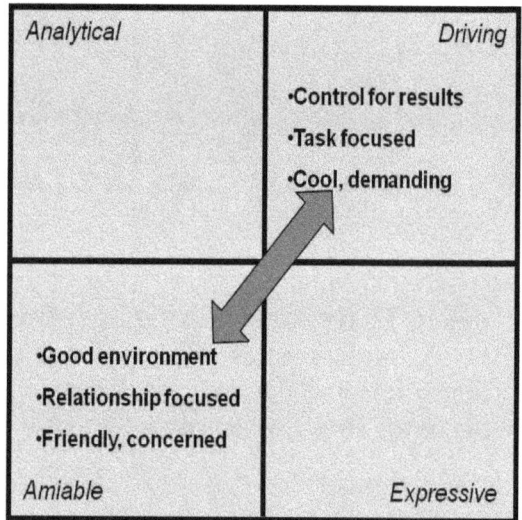

relationship. And building relationships takes conversation, which takes time that Driving Style people don't want to spend.

Because Amiable Style people are Ask Assertive, the Driving Style person tends to run over them. They might not speak up in order to prevent conflict and risk damaging what little relationship there is, but they will get even.

Driving Style with Expressive Style

Expressive style people are also Tell Assertive. As "big picture" people, they focus on how great things will be in the future, especially if you are involved with them. Their home base is below the center line so they emote with gestures, voice inflections, and facial expression. Because feelings are important to them, these Feelers make a decision based on how it feels ~~to them~~. Communicating about data and details doesn't rank high on their priority list.

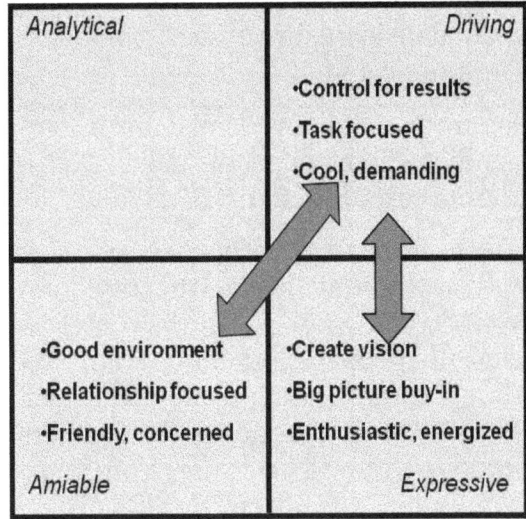

This decision making process is quite a contrast to the cool, logical, task-focused Driving style: There is plenty of room for communication difficulties.

Driving Style with Analytical Style

The Analytical Style folks are also above the line, and have no difficulties with the touchy feely stuff. They are more Ask Assertive than the Driving Style. That means they talk quietly and slowly, focusing on process (i.e., How is this going to work?).

They are focused on analyzing the data to come up with a good

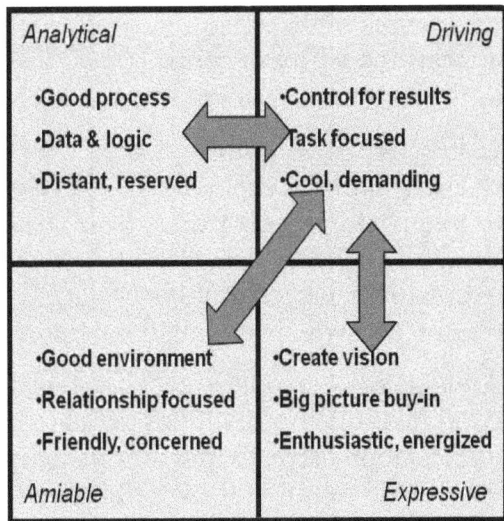

process. Tasks aren't the critical issue, process is. That means a lot of data is required to validate their thinking and should be communicated.

Do you see a high potential for miscommunication and even conflict when two people talk to each other from their different "home base" SOCIAL STYLE?

The location of your "home base" on the SOCIAL STYLE matrix can largely contribute to the miscommunications that happen. If your "home base" is near the center of the matrix, it means you're closer to people in other quadrants and should have an easier time communicating than if the intersection is far from the center. If your style is near any of the edges, more of the people you interact with will be farther from you, which makes communicating effectively difficult.

Same-Style Conflict

Conflict can also result between people of the same style. For example, Driving Style people want to be in control of situations because they are action-oriented and focused on tasks and results. Conflict can occur between two people of this style concerning who's in control and which tasks to focus on.

Expressive Style people want to create and sell their vision to others as "big picture" thinkers., Conflict can arise over which vision should be chosen and who is getting the personal approval that's needed.

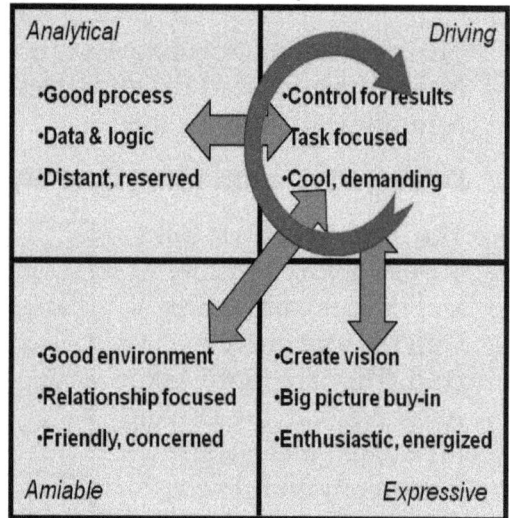

Analytical	Driving
•Good process •Data & logic •Distant, reserved	•Control for results •Task focused •Cool, demanding
•Good environment •Relationship focused •Friendly, concerned	•Create vision •Big picture buy-in •Enthusiastic, energized
Amiable	Expressive

Amiable Style people are focused on relationships. The essence of good relationships includes people's motives and feelings and interactions between and among people. Conflict can arise when various values and motives threaten the security of a trusting relationship.

Analytical Style people want an organized, detailed solution that makes sense, one based on facts, not feelings. For them, data and logic are keys to getting work done. Conflict can arise over which data is the right data and which solution is correct.

Do you see the opportunities for communication conflict due to innate differences in SOCIAL STYLE? What can be done to reduce the conflict and increase the effectiveness of all communications? Use the following three Adaptation Skills.

Adapt the Message

Most people feel more comfortable, and communicate easier with people who are near them on the SOCIAL STYLE matrix, than those who are not. For example, two people with a Driving Style will talk about tasks and not spend time with personal information. Two with an Amiable Style will touch base on their personal situation to maintain their relationship before focusing on their work issues.

What do you do if the person is not close to you on the SOCIAL STYLE matrix? Here is the beauty of understanding the model.

You can modify your behaviors *at the moment* to make other people feel more comfortable, and you can make sure you give them the information they need.

Remember, you don't have to change who you are to increase your effectiveness. You simply adapt your own behavior during the interaction.

Modify Your Assertiveness

Yes, you can modify your Assertiveness at the moment in the range from Ask Assertive to Tell Assertive. For example, you can slow down your speaking or speed it up. You can talk louder or softer. You can modify your gestures. The easiest way to get it right is to behave in the same way the person you're talking to is behaving.

Modify Your Responsiveness

Recall that the vertical axis is Responsiveness. You can temporarily modify your behavior in this dimension.

Remember, the people above the center line value data and logic. They are not comfortable with strong emoting: they are Thinkers. When interacting with people who are above the line, ask them what they think and tell them what you think.

By comparison, people below the line are Feelers. They value feelings and use them in their decision making. For below-the-line people, ask them what they feel and tell them what you feel. Vary your voice and expressions.

Deliver the Information

Whether it's making a behavior change, buying into your idea, or supporting your action plan, each SOCIAL STYLE needs to see how agreeing with you satisfies what's important to his/her style.

Those with Driving Style want to be in control of situations because they are task and results oriented. Because they want control, they like options so they can make the choice. It's all about what tasks are next on the list.

Those with Expressive Style are motivated by exciting visions they create or can buy into. They want to get others actively participating so they can have the fun of being involved and receive personal recognition for it. They are concerned about the why behind the big-picture vision or dream.

Those with Amiable Style value solid relationships in a positive human environment to get things done. As Feelers, they believe if people have good relationships and can work together well as a result, they can accomplish any task. Their main concern is, "Who will I be working with?"

Those with Analytical Style want an organized, detailed solution that makes sense. That solution must be based on facts, not feelings. For them, data and logic are keys to getting work done. They want to understand the processes that will get the right outcome, so they ask, "How will this result come about?"

The following chart summarizes this concept and identifies a key word for each style.

Key Words for Each Style:

What do you do when dealing with each SOCIAL STYLE?

Driving: Support their conclusions, be efficient with time and information, and give them choices. Cover the **What?**

Expressive: Support their big-picture dreams and intuition. Be enthusiastic and animated; provide personal testimonies. When learning something, they tend to ask someone rather than read a report. Cover the **Why?**

Amiable: Take time to support their relationships and values. Be agreeable, open, and casual. Guarantee that you'll give your personal support. Cover the **Who?**

Analytical: Support their thinking and principles. Be accurate and thorough with the details; provide data and focus on the process of **How?**

The SOCIAL STYLE model explains the concepts of Assertiveness and Responsiveness as well as adapting the message so others can hear us. Dr. Merrill also found an important third element in his research: Versatility™.

Understand Versatility

In addition to Assertiveness and Responsiveness, the third element in the SOCIAL STYLE model is Versatility.

Some people have a gift to be able to get along with those who have SOCIAL STYLEs that differ from their own. One time you see them having a great time with a group of Expressive Style people and the next time you see them, they are deep in a technical discussion with Analytical Style people. This ability to work effectively with different SOCIAL STYLEs is called Versatility.

Most of us are aware of some amount of tension when we interact with others, especially if we don't know them well. We become aware of our own tension. Do we feel comfortable with the other person? What is our confidence level? What is the potential for conflict?

This awareness of the tension, combined with our efforts to reduce it, is reflected in our Versatility at three levels: Low, Medium, and High.

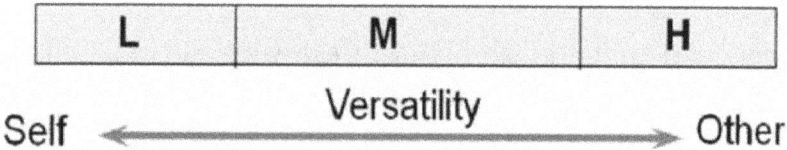

L	M	H

Self ← Versatility → Other

Measurement

Low

People at the Low Versatility level feel more comfortable around people with a SOCIAL STYLE similar to theirs. They are most concerned with their own tension or discomfort in social situations. They usually seek situations that capitalize on their technical skills, abilities, and knowledge to build mutually productive relationships.

Medium

Medium Versatility people are able to handle greater amounts of tension than those with Low Versatility. They are not only aware of their own tension but also the other person's tension. They want to make both parties comfortable in the interaction and are versatile enough to modify their behavior to be more like the other person's SOCIAL STYLE. They have the social resourcefulness to build productive relationships. This medium level of Versatility would be useful for a team lead, supervisor, or manager. In their roles, these people can't choose who they interact with by SOCIAL STYLE; their versatility has a direct correlation to their success as managers.

High

High Versatility people are highly adaptable to another person's SOCIAL STYLE. They seem most concerned with the person's tension rather than with their own. They like to make everyone feel comfortable. Many of these people are found at the higher levels in an organization. As an example, the CIO (Chief Information Officer) must have high analytical ability to do the job well but also needs to interact effectively with many different stakeholders inside and outside the company.

Personal Example:

When I was a young product manager at Hewlett Packard (HP), we had the board of directors attend a division review. In the social time before dinner, a co-worker from accounting and I found ourselves talking with Bill Hewlett, president of HP, and Earnest Arbuckle, past dean of the Stanford Business School and chairman of Wells Fargo Bank.

Needless to say, I felt intimidated in their presence. They made me feel comfortable and included. Then one of them said, "Did you see what the First National City Bank did yesterday?" The conversation floated up to a level I had no connection to. I saw they were truly highly competent men. Before long, they brought the conversation back down to my level and made me again feel like "one of the guys."

Versatility is a tremendous asset for success.
– Dick Cochran

Get Feedback on Versatility

We can get a sense of a person's Versatility by the descriptions used by people who know them.

Positive adjectives mean that even though people have a very different SOCIAL STYLE than us, they are still able to make us feel comfortable. We come away thinking, "I'd like to interact with that person again."

Negative adjectives suggest that others make us feel uncomfortable and therefore aren't versatile enough to adapt to our SOCIAL STYLE. We come away thinking, "I'd hate to deal with that person again."

Versatility Adjectives

Tell Assertiveness Negatives
- Serious
- Pushy
- Overbearing
- Rude

Ask Assertiveness Negatives
- Indecisive
- Wimpy
- Passive
- Timid

Tell Assertiveness Positives
- Independent
- Dynamic
- Driven
- Go Getter

Ask Assertiveness Positives
- Dependable
- Supportive
- Thorough
- Careful

It's not your SOCIAL STYLE that's important; it's how your behavior makes the other person feel.

That's why Versatility is important.

Components of Versatility

We relate to others in four different areas that determine our Versatility: Image, Presentation, Competence, and Feedback.

Image

Dress, grooming, and initial appearance are often critical in making good first impressions on others. Conveying the appropriate physical image for the situation is important.

Presentation

Our ability to verbally communicate with others is important, particularly in meetings and formal presentations. People are more likely to support us if we have our ideas organized, speak clearly, and use a vocabulary appropriate to the circumstances.

Competence

Competence is an evaluation of a number of capacities that affect others' abilities to achieve their own goals. It includes our dependability, perseverance, and flexibility. It also gauges our level of optimism and ability to help solve problems as well as think creatively.

Feedback

Using clear and accurate verbal and nonverbal information or signals to promote maximum understanding helps others have confidence in us. By checking for understanding and being sensitive to the signals others are sending, we can increase the support and respect we receive from others.

Increasing Versatility

All of these capacities can be developed over time, thus leading to increased Versatility. So take these actions that will directly boost your Versatility and make other people feel more comfortable.

Know Yourself: Build on your strengths; minimize your weaknesses.

Control Yourself: Act appropriately and give people a little time to get to know you.

Know Others: Be observant to others' SOCIAL STYLE and needs.

Do Something for Others: Step out of your comfort zone and move closer to theirs.

These actions work together to make people feel more comfortable, increase trust, and give you more opportunities to work successfully with everyone.

Use SOCIAL STYLE Emulation

Are you familiar with the term "emulation" from the computer world? For example, an Apple computer can emulate a PC. That means it acts like a PC and runs PC programs, but it doesn't become a PC.

Similarly, you can emulate a different SOCIAL STYLE than your own for a short time. When you do, you can become more successful working with a person of that Style. You'll make that person feel more comfortable and therefore you'll have a much better chance of having a successful interaction. You don't have to become that Style; you simply modify your behavior while interacting with that person.

Dick's Rule:

If you feel uncomfortable with the changes you made in your behavior to make the other person feel comfortable, you are emulating the SOCIAL STYLE just right.

Platinum Rule

One guideline that many have grown up with is the Golden Rule: "Do unto others as you would have them do unto you." As Tony Alessandra and Michael O'Connor point out in their book *The Platinum Rule*, the Golden Rule has the potential for communications conflict. If you treat others like your SOCIAL STYLE and they are somewhere else on the SOCIAL STYLE matrix, the interaction will likely cause conflict.

The Platinum Rule they created means, in short, learning to understand other people and then handling them in a way that's best for them, not just for you. I suggest using a modified version of it.

Dick's Platinum Rule:

*Do unto others as **they** want to be done unto.*

Using SOCIAL STYLEs is fundamental to any interaction—at work, at home, and in social situations.

From my experience and observation, people are born with their own SOCIAL STYLE. If you have children, is their Style the same as yours? The answer is probably "no." Does that explain some of the conflicts you experience? Likely. If you have a spouse or significant other, is that person's SOCIAL STYLE the same as yours? The answer again is probably "no." Even worse, you're attracted to that person because he or she has the SOCIAL STYLE traits you don't have. This is great for creating a more complete team, but it also is a recipe for built-in conflict.

Your SOCIAL STYLEs, which are observable, explain much of the conflict that happens when communicating. The good news is that it's not your fault. It's not what you said; it's the way you said it. And more good news is this: You can adapt the delivery of your message and effectively bridge the communications gap.

Applications: *Adapt the Message*

Now that you understand the differences in SOCIAL STYLE and the importance of Versatility: look at where and how you can use the knowledge to be more effective. In the discussion that follows, let's assume you're initiating an interaction with a specific outcome in mind.

One-On-One Communications

Using SOCIAL STYLE is most effective in this situation because you only have to adapt the message to the other person's Style. There are three situations to focus on—face to face, voice to voice, and screen to screen.

Face to Face

This gives you the most information on others' SOCIAL STYLE. You can see their facial expressions and body language: e.g., how they carry themselves, how they gesture, etc. Face to face gives you maximum ability to adapt your message. You can modify your voice in volume, pace, and tone. You can change your body language to be more like theirs: bigger or smaller gestures, more assertive or less assertive posture. Face to face also gives you the most feedback on how you are doing.

For Example:

Amiable Style people speaking to Driving Style people might make sure they speak directly and to the point. They would talk fast and offer Driving Style people several options to let them make the choice and be in control. Anallytical Style people speaking to Expressive Style people would talk faster, showing excitement and enthusiasm in both their voice and gestures. They would give the Expressive Style people the "big picture" explanation about why they were having a particular conversation.

Voice to Voice

Many times you don't get to be face to face but have to talk on the phone. The other person can be miles, even countries, away. This situation is more difficult than face to face because you lose visual information when communicating, but you can still apply the SOCIAL STYLE concept.

If you have ever worked at a help desk or in customer service, you can quickly tell differences in people's SOCIAL STYLEs. What does the Driving Style sound like? "I need you to fix this!" They are firm, fast-talking, and to the point. They want to know what you are going to do and by when. How about Amiable Style people? They talk softly and ask questions. Their request sounds like this: "I hate to bother you, but I have a problem. I need to find someone to help me." It's quite different than Driving Style.

Each SOCIAL STYLE needs its Key Word Question answered. In the help desk example, the Driving Style wants to know what's going to be done and by when. The Expressive Style wants to know why it happened. The Amiable Style needs to know who, specifically, will help. And the Analytical Style wants to know how the process will work.

Screen to Screen

This refers to email, instant messaging, texting, and any written documentation. Screen-to-screen communication is even more difficult than the others because both the visual and the audio inputs are missing. However, the point is still the same. Each person needs to recognize the appropriate Key Words in Assertiveness and Responsiveness for their "home base" on the SOCIAL STYLE matrix. Each person needs his or her Key Word Question answered: What? Why? Who? How?

In Groups

When interacting with a group of people or running a meeting, you usually have more than one SOCIAL STYLE present. You can be face to face, voice to voice, or screen to screen. For groups, the important considerations are content and the sequence of presenting that content.

Content

Since each Style needs to get the respective Key Word Question answered, you need to cover the What? Why? Who? and How? The problem is that most people structure a presentation based on their own "home base" SOCIAL STYLE. They unconsciously focus on answering their own Key Word Question first when organizing the presentation. People naturally address what's important to them.

For example, say you're in a meeting in which someone presented a plan for a project and after the meeting, you hear people say, "That plan will never fly. The person has no idea who will do it." Or others say, "That will never work. The person has no idea how it will get done." This means those making these statements never received the information that's important to them in the meeting. Make sure you answer all four Key Word Questions to get buy-in from all SOCIAL STYLEs.

Sequence

Have you ever had someone hijack your meeting? Our Tell Assertive friends—the Driving Style and Expressive Style—get impatient if they don't get their questions answered early in the meeting. They will interrupt the flow to get what they need, and you lose control of the meeting. For example, say the person making the presentation started off with the Who and the How. Interrupting, the Expressive Style says, "Wait a minute. Why are we worrying about how to do it? We have no idea why we are even talking about this. What's the big picture?"

Because the sequence is important, I suggest going clockwise around the matrix. Start with What, then Why, then Who, and finally How. This will satisfy our Tell Assertive friends on the right. Our Ask Assertive friends are polite and won't interrupt. Instead, they'll wait for you to cover the Key Word Question. But if you fail to do it, you won't get their buy-in.

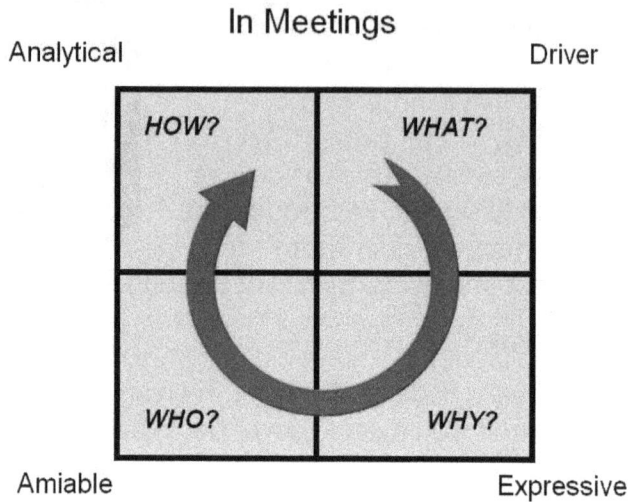

In Meetings

Analytical

Driver

HOW?	WHAT?
WHO?	WHY?

Amiable

Expressive

> **Note:** *For screen to screen, the sequence of the content also matters. This refers to any written material: emails, webinars, manuals, sales literature, training materials, etc.*

SOCIAL STYLE is especially important in emails because if people don't get their Key Word Question answered in a timely fashion, they stop reading and hit the "delete" key. Here is a simple Key Word Questions template with these four headings to fill in.

What?

Why?

Who?

How?

Manager / Supervisor

Our individual SOCIAL STYLE and our Versatility play an important role in how we manage others. We wrongly assume that our "position power" is all that's important. At the same time, we wonder and complain about lack of commitment and buy-in from the people who work for us.

First, know your own SOCIAL STYLE. Each one has a strength that's valuable, but that can be overdone. The Driving Style can be overbearing. The Expressive Style may not stay focused. The Amiable Style may be too worried about relationships to get the task done. The Analytical Style person can over analyze. Observe how others perceive your Style-related behaviors.

Second, use Versatility to interact with each of your direct reports from the context of Style. Present your requests emphasizing what's important to them.

Your team, no matter what their Style, can provide the work you want. The Style most like yours will be easier for you because you don't have to change your normal approach. But if you want buy-in and commitment from the other three SOCIAL STYLEs, making the small change in behavior to fit their Style will pay off.

Project Manager / Team Lead

Team leaders usually don't have the power that managers do to hire and fire; therefore, persuasion becomes highly important. The more versatile you are, the higher the chance you'll get positive responses to your requests. So it makes sense to always frame the request in the SOCIAL STYLE of the person you're asking rather than using your natural approach. Emulation works.

Teams can be even more effective when everyone on the team is aware of and uses the SOCIAL STYLE model. You increase communication content and reduce time spent trying to figure out what the other person meant. For example, when an Analytical Style person and an Expressive Style person interact using these skills, the Expressive Style person provides the data the Analytical Style needs and the Analytical Style person provides the "big picture" the Expressive Style needs: Interaction completed!

Team Member / Co-worker / Direct Report

Being a direct report has the unique responsibility of dealing with your boss. It's important to figure out that person's SOCIAL STYLE because he or she has position power. Don't expect your boss to adapt to your Style; adaptation will probably be up to you.

For example, if your boss is an Analytical Style, he or she will probably want status reports with detail, data, and backup information. By comparison, an Expressive Style boss will want a report of the "big picture," trusting you to be handling the details.

As a team member, many times you have to interact with other team members to get their support, assistance, or results from their effort. Using your versatility and treating them according to the needs of their SOCIAL STYLE can be like building a bank account of trust. That way, you can call on that account when you need it most.

Review

> ➤ Know that you have a SOCIAL STYLE that's visible to others.

> ➤ Adapt the delivery of your message to match the other person's SOCIAL STYLE.

> ➤ Use your SOCIAL STYLE skills to increase the effectiveness of your interactions.

> ➤ Increase your Versatility; it's the key to true success.

> ➤ Use emulation to adapt to another's SOCIAL STYLE.

How do I get people to focus on the Real Issue?

We spend a big part of our lives dealing with issues. I developed a metaphor that we are all on a journey through the "cow pasture" of life. Take a minute and think about what your ideal cow pasture would look like.

Mine has lush green grass, beautiful cows, rolling hills with trees and water. It's a pretty nice picture. Our goal in life is to make our way across the cow pasture avoiding the piles of manure (cow patties) whenever possible. We enjoy the trip and finally end up on the other side of the pasture.

In this metaphorical cow pasture of life, what's the problem? Unfortunately, there are flying cows. So no matter how careful we are, cow's random airborne projectiles (c.r.a.p.) land on us, and we have to deal with them.

C.R.A.P. Happens

We encounter cow patties (challenges) in both our personal and business lives. They disrupt us emotionally while taking valuable resources to resolve them.

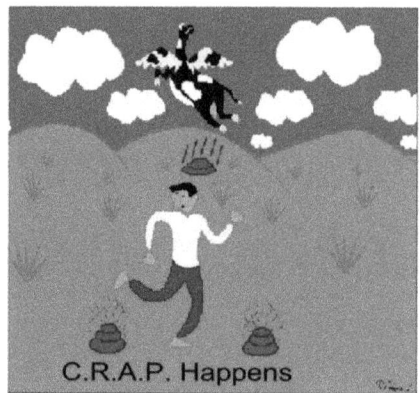

C.R.A.P. Happens

Cow's Random Airborne Projectiles

When we encounter the cow patties of life, we go through the same process in dealing with them. This Problem-Solving Process applies whether we are at work, in our social situations, or at home with our families. Some people get stuck in the process; others breeze right through it.

How fast we resolve any cow patty issue depends on our personality and the patty's size. By understanding the Problem-Solving Process and learning how to help move through it, we can significantly reduce the emotional energy and unproductive time spent whining, moaning and groaning about that patty. We get on with living our lives.

Let's look at how the Problem-Solving Process can help.

Know the Problem-Solving Process

The first phase in the Process is Venting, that is, we whine, moan and groan about the issue. We let off steam from the stress and hassles of having to deal with the problem. At some point, we realize that the cow patty won't go away. Yes, we have to deal with it.

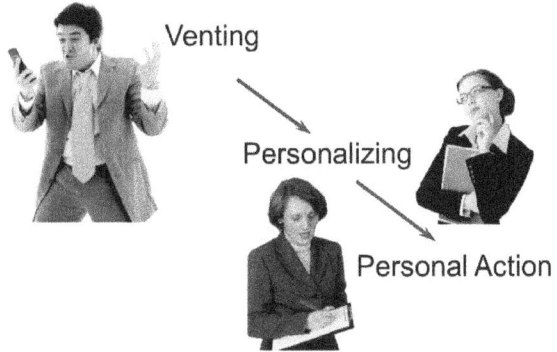

Venting

Personalizing

Personal Action

From there, we move to Personalizing. We try to figure out what we can do to resolve the issue. We take ownership for what we can do about the issue. We start the Problem-Solving Process and eventually arrive at a solution.

We then move to the third phase, which is Personal Action. Just knowing what to do isn't enough; we need to create detailed action steps that will successfully carry out our plan.

Let's look at an example:

Problem-Solving Example:

I'm so darned mad. The company has changed its vacation policy so I can't carry over my unused vacation. Now I'm going to lose it. I was just trying to be a good team player and not take vacation until the project was finished. The managers don't care about me. It's always about the bottom line. How could I have been so stupid as to trust them?

What can I do? I can't change management. But I can control when I take my vacation. I'll do it when I want, not when they want.

Here's what I'll do. Tonight, I'll sit down with my family and decide when and where we're going to go on vacation. Then tomorrow, I'll put in my request to HR.

In this example, our unhappy employee went through all three phases in a fairly linear and timely fashion. Many times in real life, it's not this simple.

We can spend a lot of time Venting. Personalizing doesn't necessarily come quickly or easily. If we can reduce the time we or others spend Venting, we can get to Personal Action sooner and use that time for more productive activities.

Let's detail the Problem-Solving Process so we can help ourselves and others move through it more effectively.

Become Aware of a Problem

We first have to become aware there is a problem—a cow patty. Sometimes it just falls from the sky. But sometimes it's not so obvious. We don't know what's wrong, but we have thoughts and feelings that suggest something's not quite right.

Symptoms:

- Unhappy
- Bored
- Hurt
- Angry

- Upset
- Tired
- Confused
- Sad

These thoughts and feelings convey there's an issue—a cow patty—to deal with. Also, we can notice these behaviors in others and recognize they also have a cow patty to deal with. We choose whether or not to get involved.

Venting

When first encountering the cow patty, we tend to Vent; we whine, moan, and groan. Blowing off steam is a normal part of the Problem-Solving Process. It does work to reduce our stress.

There are two types of Venting: Externalizing and Internalizing. Recognizing each helps identify where someone is in the Problem-Solving Process. Remember, the goal is to get to problem solving sooner and arrive at solutions faster.

Externalizing

Externalizing means that someone or something external to us is causing the problem. We blame everything outside of ourselves—that is, we blame "them" or "you" or "it" or anything we think caused the cow patty. We may say, "It's 'their' fault entirely."

Internalizing

Internalizing means that something internal to us caused the problem. We use words such as "I" or "my" or "me" plus blameful sentences such as, "How could I have been so stupid?" and "It's all my fault."

Personalizing

At some point after venting for a while, we realize the "cow patty" won't go away, so we have to deal with the issue at hand. This second step, Personalizing, involves taking personal responsibility to do something that's within our control. This is where problem solving happens.

Specifically, we start looking for causes. We explore options and seek alternatives and actions that move us toward solving the problem. We realize we can only control ourselves. So we look for what we, personally, can do. At this point, we arrive at a plan for resolving the issue—the cow patty.

Personal Action

Of course, only knowing what to do isn't enough. How many times have we said, "Yes, I know what to do; I just haven't done it"?

The third step is to move toward a Personal Action plan. This means creating steps, actions, and timing to resolve the issue. We put in place the action steps and the timing to implement our Problem-Solving plan.

Listen for Word Clues

The words people use tell us where they are in the Problem-Solving Process. From what they say, are they Venting, Internalizing, or Externalizing? Are they Personalizing, or are they Action Planning?

We can listen for the words used. Blame words used with I, me, we, or my would indicate Internalizing. Blame words used with they, them, or someone else would indicate Externalizing. Personalizing is tricky because we hear internal action words such as "I" or "me," and we also hear action concepts or words such as "do."

By comparison, in Action Planning, we hear the words or specifics around what and when. In this example, the words tell you where this employee is in the Problem-Solving Process? Pick them out.

Example: Identifying one's place in the Problem-Solving Process

I can't understand why I haven't gotten a raise or a promotion. I've been here a long time. I think I do my work as well as anyone else. I must have offended someone in management. (PAUSE) I know this job backward and forward. Basically, I'm just bored. I need something more stimulating. I'll go see the people in Human Resources tomorrow.

– Unhappy employee

Debriefing this example:

I can't understand why I haven't gotten a raise or a promotion (from them—Externalizing). I've been here a long time (should be long enough). I think I do my work as well as anyone else. (I'm not being fairly treated, by them—Externalizing.) I must have offended someone in management. (It's my fault—

51

Internalizing.) (PAUSE) I know this job backward and forward. Basically, I'm just bored. I need something more stimulating. (Personalizing) I'll go see the people in Human Resources tomorrow. (Action Planning)

It's helpful to know where we are or where the other person is in the process. We often turn to Venting to blow off steam and reduce the stress caused by the current cow patty. Personalizing is a conscious effort to use that "steam" to affect a change. Stated another way, Venting is reacting negatively to stress. Personalizing is reacting positively to stress.

Venting *hinders* the Problem-Solving Process.

Personalizing *promotes* the Problem-Solving Process.

As individuals, we move through the Problem-Solving Process at different rates. Sometimes we need to spend more time Venting. Sometimes it helps to air our emotions to someone else.

So the question becomes this: How do we reduce unproductive Venting and move quickly to the positive Personalizing part of the process?

Ask the Un-Ableness Question

When we are Venting, it's usually because we don't see a solution to the cow patty. There is a deficit. There is something we are unable to do at the moment. Yes, it feels good to whine and moan and groan, but if we could see a solution, we'd usually take it. We need a way to help move us from Venting to Personalizing. The tool to do that is the Un-Ableness Question.

For Ourselves

When you find yourself venting, stop and ask yourself this question.

"What is it I am unable to do, that

if I could do it, would solve the problem?"

This is the magic question—not blaming or judgmental. It just asks what you are unable to do at the moment. When you use this tool, you will actually hear and feel the shift from Venting to Personalizing.

For Others One-On-One

Many times people bring us problems. When I was a manager, it felt as if staff members were bringing their problems on a silver tray and asking me to take them on. And I used to do it a lot. I thought I was helping.

More than that, I decided it was easier to do it than to manage them to solve the problem themselves. In fact, I thought they would like me more and see me as a hero. But it never worked out that way. I finally realized two things. First, I never solved the problem adequately enough for them, so they weren't happy with me. Second, I was doing all the work.

We need to make sure the other person retains ownership of the problem. We simply change the "I" to "you" and the Un-Ableness question becomes:

"What is it YOU are unable to do, that

if YOU could do it, would solve the problem?"

Memorize this question. Use it often to help people discover the real problem to focus on. Many times when people Vent, they aren't focusing on their real problem. So when they pause for a breath, ask them this question. You'll actually see them shift their brain from Venting to Personalizing.

I've found that using a hand gesture while asking this question gives me something to do as I connect with the other person. I use both hands in an open, supportive, and socially acceptable hand gesture.

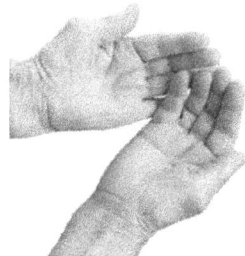

53

For Groups and Teams

Have you ever seen a group meeting turn into an "ain't it awful" session? At times, the cow patty does affect the whole team. Each member whines, moans, and groans about it: Nothing gets done!

Again, this is a normal part of the Problem-Solving Process. But after a brief time, it's important to refocus the team as a unit. The tool to use is the Un-Ableness question. You or someone can speak up at the meeting and say:

> **"What is it WE are unable to do, that**
>
> **if WE could do it, would solve the problem?"**

It's amazing to see the whole group shift from Venting to Personalizing and begin solving the problem.

Limit Victim Behavior

Some people seem to handle the cow patties of life more effectively than others. They Vent, but they don't get bogged down in it. They quickly move on to Personalizing and developing a solution, then they take Personal Action. That's how these self-empowered people handle the cow patties of life.

If we get wrapped up in Venting, we can't see the options and get stuck. It's called Victim Behavior.

This term is not meant to be judgmental. We believe most people are doing the best they can at the moment. Remember that Venting is a natural and normal part of the Problem-Solving Process. It simply takes time for people to work through it. Said another way, some cow patties take longer to process.

Do recognize this kind of behavior, though, because when people are stuck Venting, they are not problem solving and moving

forward. Let's define it, see how to test for it, and then discuss what to do about it.

Definition of Victim Behavior:

When someone is asked the Un-Ableness Question and is unwilling to Personalize and continues to Vent, watch out. That person is exhibiting Victim Behavior.

Test for Victim Behavior

The way you test for Victim Behavior is to ask those people the Un-Ableness question. If they continue to Vent, you ask it again. They don't even register the question and continue to Vent. If, after the third time you ask, and they continue to Vent, then take it as an indication they're not ready to move to Personalizing.

You now have two action choices:

First: If you need to solve the problem quickly, and time is of the essence, find alternative resources to help you. This person isn't able to do it at the moment.

Second: If the relationship is important, spend the time with this person listening and supporting the relationship even though it will probably not move to Personalizing.

Limiting the Venting Virus

When someone is Venting, that person's stress level goes down, which is what venting is supposed to accomplish. But what's happening to the stress levels of the people around them? They go up. And with stress going up for the team, productivity goes down. So we don't want someone's Venting to infect the others.

If you put in place the following two rules and call them team norms, you can support the normal Venting process. In addition, you can lower the stress level for the entire team, thereby keeping up its productivity.

Rules for Reducing Venting Stress on Others

> *1. Vent in semi-private.*
>
> *2. Ask permission first.*

First, to reduce venting stress on others, ask the team to agree not to vent in public. That includes the middle of the cafeteria, in a team meeting, or anywhere that others will overhear. Instead, use your office, a conference room, or the outdoors. So find a semi-private place where Venting won't affect others.

Second, the team agrees to ask permission of the listener before launching off. The request might sound like this: "Hey Dick, do you have a few minutes? I need to vent."

Notice the two important issues here. You want to be supportive and just listen to the Venting. If you don't have time, you can't be supportive. But you can schedule another time to give your full attention to the other person.

Another important benefit is reminding those who are Venting that they are in a Problem-Solving Process. Explain that Venting should lead to Personalizing and then to Action Planning. This will shorten the time spent Venting.

Constant Venting

Some people you encounter seem to always Vent. They don't even want to Personalize or Take Action. The Un-Ableness question doesn't work with these people. So you need to confront them and ask them for a behavior change. (You'll find formats for that in a later section.)

Personalizing

Venting for most people is an unconscious reaction to encountering a cow patty. Usually, you initiate the transition from Venting to Personalizing with the Un-Ableness Question, which involves asking people to identify what they're unable to do.

You likely won't get a quick, clear response because they haven't been thinking about that. Instead, they've been busy Venting.

Don't lose sight of your task, which is to listen closely and pick out exactly what they are unable to do.

Restate Un-Ableness

There is no point spending time and effort working on the wrong problem. Naturally, you want confirmation that you got it right.

Once you think you know what they're unable to do, confirm it by restating what you heard. "So, you are unable to ...." Often you'll get the response, "No, that's not it," and they start Venting again.

So ask the question again, listen, and again restate the point of un-ableness you heard. "So, you are unable to . . ." Restating works in a one-on-one situation and also applies when interacting with a team or group. Your goal is to identify one issue to take to the next step in the Problem-Solving Process.

Explore Options and Solutions

Once you have the issue identified, begin developing a solution or steps to move the person forward. This is a free-flowing discussion in which you examine past information. Together, you explore options, look for root causes, brainstorm solutions, evaluate alternatives, and prioritize or rank them: You end up choosing a course of action.

You may also discover something else is the real issue. It's okay to shift to that; however, be sure to test it by restating the un-ableness issue and getting confirmation that it has become the point of focus.

It's possible there is no solution to the issue. If so, you then need to explain the concept of the three options.

The Three Options

Sometimes people focus on trying to solve a problem that can't be solved, whining, moaning, and groaning about it. They even explore options, only to realize that there is no solution. This creates a disempowering feeling and much frustration. They believe they're trapped in a situation.

Three Options Example:

You are a good team payer working on an important project. You haven't taken your vacation time in two years because you don't want to negatively affect the project. And the project is moving to completion.

You get the memo or announcement that the company has changed its vacation policy, and now you will lose your unused vacation. You vent. "Darned company managers; they don't care. How could I be so stupid trusting them?"

You ask yourself the Un-Ableness Question. The answer is "I am unable to get the company to go back to the old policy." You are frustrated, so you whine, moan, and groan some more. You are stuck. You have probably seen people who have been venting for months or years about some issue. Whenever you have to deal with one of life's cow patties, you always have three options.

Option 1. Find a solution that resolves the issue (the primary focus of this handbook).

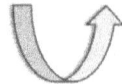

Option 2. Change yourself. If you can't change the issue, you can change your attachment to it.

Option 3. Remove yourself from the situation.

Costs associated with all of these options:

Option 1, you have to spend time and energy to find the solution. Getting the desired changes may require confronting someone.

Option 2, it's not easy to change your attachment for an issue labeled a cow patty. You can change how you "hold" it; you don't have to agree with it or condone it. But you do have to accept it and get on with your life. "It is what it is."

Option 3 comes into play when you declare, "I can't change it, and I can't accept it." Well, you can always remove yourself from the situation. Sometimes the cost is high, such as leaving a job or a relationship. But you always have this option.

In the example of the change in vacation policy:

Option 1 doesn't work.

Option 3 may be too extreme over its vacation policy. So . . ..

Option 2 seems like the best choice. You don't have to like it or even agree with it; you just have to accept "that's the way it is" and let it go. Don't spend more time and energy whining, moaning, and groaning. Just get on with life.

No matter which option you choose in the Personalizing part of the Problem-Solving Process, your goal is to arrive at an action point with an understanding of what needs to be done. Then you'll take one more step—Personal Action.

Take Personal Action

simply knowing the solution to a problem is not enough. You know what to do, but don't act? You say, "I know I should eat better, but . . .." "I know I should exercise more, but . . .."

Here's how to get over that hurdle of inaction.

4Ws are the Key

Asking the 4Ws forces others to be specific about their commitments and think about things that will interfere with keeping them.

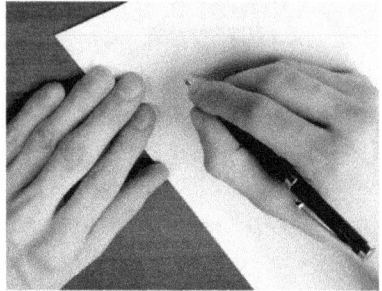

Who?

What?

When?

Where?

One of my colleagues, Tom Dearth, refers to himself as Mr. Specificity. Because much miscommunication is caused by people not being specific enough, he suggests using the word "specifically" when asking for the 4Ws

"Who, specifically, is involved?"

"What, specifically, are you going to do?"

"When, specifically, is it going to happen?"

"Where, specifically, will action take place?"

In the following example assume a co-worker is asking me to come in on the weekend to help out. That person needs to ask all four questions because each can turn up a "no."

4Ws Example:

Who? *"Dick, we need you to come in this weekend and help rearrange the new office." "Hey, I'm a team player you can count on me!"*

What? *"We need you to help carry the copy machine up to the second floor." "Oh, wow. I'd love to help but my back keeps going out. I guess I can't do it."*

When? *"We're all meeting at 10:00 a.m. on Saturday." "Oh, 10:00, gee, my daughter's soccer final is that morning. I can't help after all."*

Where? *"We will be at the new office." "Wow, that's clear across town. Driving back and forth is a big chunk out of our family time that I can't afford to take. Sorry."*

By asking the 4Ws whenever others say "yes" to your request, you significantly increase the probability they will carry through with their commitment.

If you have doubts about them meeting the commitment, then you can increase the chance of success by putting in sub-milestones, each with their own set of 4Ws.

Ask yourself the 4Ws

This is a good way to ensure yourself and others that you can follow through on your commitments.

Get and Give 4Ws

Making Commitments Happen:

Applying the 4Ws:

1. **Get** *the 4Ws whenever someone says yes to your request. It increases the chances they will take follow-through action.*

2. **Give** *the 4Ws whenever you say yes to a request. Then you'll make sure you can follow through.*

One measure of emotional health is how directly you process the "cow patties" of life. Of course, each person has a different speed; and the size of the "cow patty" makes a great difference.

But in general, the faster you move through the steps in the Problem-Solving Process, the more free time you have between "cow patties." Realize that C.R.A.P. will happen, so be ready to use the Problem-Solving Process to handle the stages quickly. You can also help others identify and deal with their cow patties.

Become the Caring Consultant

Next, let's focus on improving morale on the team and help others move through the Problem-Solving Process. We will also examine what to do when people bring us their problems. We can apply the concepts to make the Problem-Solving Process work to realize more complete solutions.

Sometimes people create problems and try to have others take care of their issue. But remember, everyone has options and can choose whether or not to get involved.

You Have a Choice

Your first choice is **Apathy**. I call this approach the Disinterested Bystander, whose statement is, "It's not my battle." This stance keeps you from getting involved at all. However, consider the two disadvantages with this approach:

    A. It doesn't help solve the problem.

    B. People don't feel supported.

A second choice is **Sympathy**. I call this approach the Misguided Hero or Heroine, whose statement is "There must be a way to fix it, and it's up to me to find it." These people are the rescuers. They take on other people's problems and work diligently to solve them. By the way, new managers can sometimes fall into this trap because it's often easier to solve the problems than manage the people. This choice also has two disadvantages:

    A. It sucks you into spending time and energy developing a solution the key person isn't happy with.

    B. It removes the person from any responsibility or ownership of the problem.

A third choice is **Empathy**. I call this approach the Caring Consultant whose statement is, "It's your problem, but I will help you find a solution." It keeps the ownership of the problem with the other person, but it supports that person by helping find a solution.

Pulling all of this together, let's see how the concepts and tools discussed can work. Using the Un-Ableness Question, Re-stating Un-Ableness, the Three Choices, and 4Ws allow you to become the Caring Consultant. Most important, it helps the other person through the Problem-Solving Process.

Use the Listening Process

The Problem-Solving Process has been described as a linear series of events. But in real life, people don't go through this process in a linear fashion. It's seldom as simple as "ask the Un-Ableness question and get the answer," and then expect to be home free with the 4Ws.

Here is a diagram of what actually happens:

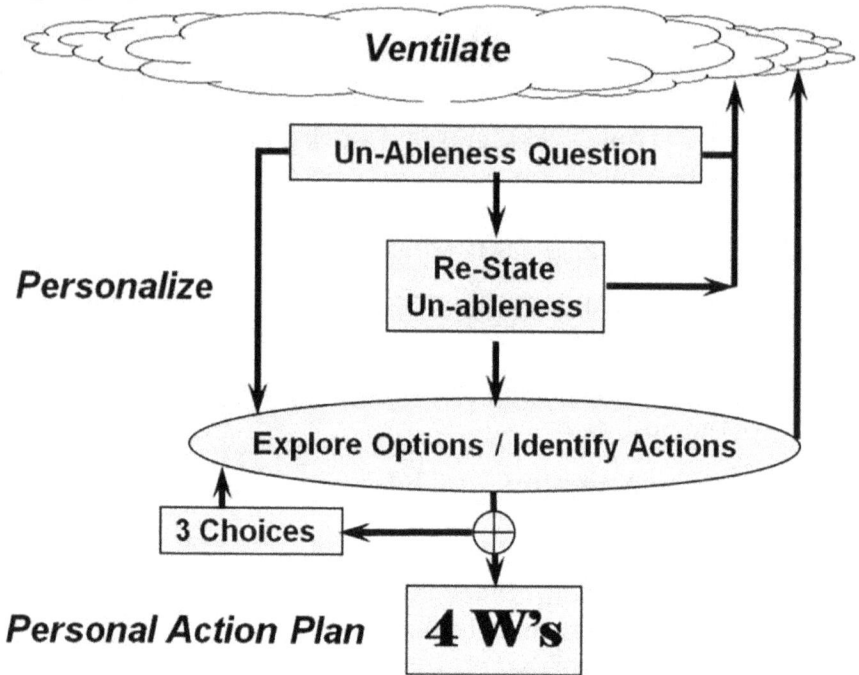

Your job as the Caring Consultant is to help others move through the Problem-Solving Process and come up with an Action Plan, knowing it can be like herding cats. You can only use the four tools shown in the diagram. Let's step through the process.

Determining Un-Ableness

Here's the scenario: People Vent, so you use your supportive listening skills and then ask the Un-Ableness Question. Afterward, several things can happen including:

They continue to Vent, you continue to ask until you think you hear what they are unable to do. Then you test it by re-stating it. They say, "Yes, that's what I am unable to do." You then move to Personalizing and exploring options.

They say, "I don't know what I am unable to do!" Sometimes people need your help to identify exactly what they are unable to do. From what you heard during their Venting, you can make suggestions. They may jump back to Venting. They may even agree with you. You test it by restating what they said they're unable to do. If they jump back to Venting, you re-test until they say, "Yes, that's what I am unable to do." You then move on to exploring options and solutions.

Getting to the Real Issue:

Unfortunately, most of the time, people don't Vent about the real problem. They Vent about something else. It might be related, but it's not the real issue. They likely don't do it on purpose, so you help them clarify the real issue. The tool to use is the Un-Ableness Question. You will likely need to ask it several times to peel back the layers of the onion.

Here's an example: Emily vents, saying, "I'm so unhappy with this job. I think I do my work as well as anyone else. But everyone else makes more money than I do. My boss says she will help me get more, but I haven't seen anything yet."

You ask, "What is it that you are unable to do, that if you could do it, would solve the problem?"

By now, you think you know the problem and several options to suggest. One is to just get over it. Another is to find comparison salaries to show Emily she's not underpaid. Caution: Don't go there!

You again ask the Un-Ableness Question. Emily answers, "I'm unable to get my boss up off her rear end to help me!"

You ask again in a caring way. "So Emily, what is it you are unable to do, that if you could do it, would solve this problem?"

Emily pauses. "What am I unable to do? What am I unable to do? I guess I am really unable to tell my family I have to quit this job and find other work."

Wow, the real issue is a lot different from where she started. But this is the issue Emily needs your help with. The other tools you have can take her through the Problem-Solving Process toward starting an Action Plan.

Exploring Options and Solutions

Finally, you both agree on what the issue is. Until now, you've only been asking the Un-Ableness Question, listening, and re-stating it. Now, you have a conversation in which you explore action options, identify causes, and discuss solutions together. The goal is for the other person to identify an action step he/she can own and be willing to implement.

Caution: Don't try to sell your solution to those you're helping. Their action step may not be a total solution. But that's okay. They're moving in the right direction. Remember, you are helping them define their problems and take their action steps. Let them discover for themselves that a solution won't work (if that's true).

The Three Choices

Change it: In the exploring process, it may become evident they can't change anything. (Remember the example of trying to change the company vacation policy?) So you would present the other two options: Change yourself or Remove yourself.

Whichever option they choose, you go back to the Exploring Options/Identify Actions portion of the Problem-Solving Process.

Change yourself: Changing yourself doesn't mean you have to change who you are; rather, you have to change your attachment to having a solution. This means accepting the issue as it is—letting it go and getting on with your life. You don't have to agree with it or condone it; you simply let it go.

Letting go is not easy. You still need to be the Caring Consultant and help others determine specifically what they need to do to "let it go." Sometimes the actions may be symbolic (e.g., writing down the issue on a piece of paper and then burning the paper). Your goal is to determine specific actions and then create a time-line so they can recognize when the letting go is complete.

Remove yourself: Each choice has a cost associated with it. Removing yourself may be the highest cost option of them all. Remember, your goal is to determine the specific actions and timing they need to accomplish this. It may be as simple as never putting themselves in a specific situation or as major as starting the process of finding a different position within the company.

Stopping the negative complainers:

Some people constantly complain about their job or the company. They are always whining, moaning, and groaning. What do you do? Confront them (see later section on this) and present the Remove Yourself option to them. They'll usually come back with comments about it being too costly for them to leave, or it's valuable to stay (e.g., "It'll be only two years until I retire with a full pension"). You can show them they made a conscious, considered choice and decided to stay and they can stop whining, moaning, and groaning because they made the choice.

Get the 4Ws

Once you have gotten to the point of the person identifying and agreeing on the action steps, it's time to develop his/her action plan. This is necessary because only knowing something needs to be done isn't enough to get it to happen.

Who, specifically, is involved?

What, specifically, will be done?

When, specifically, will the steps happen?

Where, specifically, will actions take place?

At this point, you have become the successful Caring Consultant.

Applications – The Real Issue

Helping Ourselves

There are times when we have to handle CRAP. Sometimes we find ourselves stuck Venting. But if we stop and ask ourselves the Un-Ableness Question, it will un-stick us, allowing us to move to Personalizing and then Action Planning. We always have the three choices. And we can commit to give and get the 4Ws.

Helping Others

When people bring you problems, or cow patties, you can be supportive and help them find solutions to their problems. Unfortunately, you may be a rescuer who loves to solve problems for others because you believe it makes them love and respect you. What actually happens? You go off and solve the problem, coming up with a great, creative solution and then you present it, but the other person doesn't like it. "It's not what I want." You've just wasted your time doing all that work, and in the end the other person wasn't happy with your solution; you didn't get the love and respect you wanted.

Don't do this anymore. Let others own the solutions to their problems. You can be the Caring Consultant and help with the Un-Ableness Question and the 4Ws, but don't take on the problem yourself.

Helping a Team

Teams go through the same Problem-Solving Process as individuals, so apply the Un-Ableness Question and the 4Ws work with your team.

Teach the team the Problem-Solving Process and the Three Choices. Make sure that team norms include giving and getting the 4Ws and asking permission to Vent. When you do, this will increase the effectiveness of the whole team.

When you start using the Un-Ableness Question with people on the team, you may find this interesting phenomenon: Team members realize that when they come to you to Vent, you will consistently ask them the un-ableness question.

The dialogue might sound like this:

"Hi Dick, do you have a minute, I need to vent?"
"Sure."
"But you're going to ask me that Un-Ableness Question, aren't you?"
"Yes, I am."
"Well, then, let's just skip to what am I unable to do."

Think of how much time can be saved when your team members have the skills to work more effectively with each other.

Review

> ➢ C.R.A.P. happens.
> ➢ We always have three choices.
> ➢ The Un-Ableness Question identifies the real issue.
> ➢ The 4Ws solidify the action.

How do I get people to better work with me?

Trust is a quality we earn through our interactions with others. The premise is this: If people trust us, they are more likely to do what we ask, support us, and have a more effective and productive working relationship with us.

This section addresses how to build trust in the first place and how to maintain it in the long run. Trust varies over time in our relationships. Sometimes we start out with a high level of trust and then we do something uncaring that immediately lowers the trust level. How can we earn back the trust?

Let's find out how we can apply the skills we're learning to be even more effective in building trust with others.

Understand the Trust Meter

We all have a built-in trust meter that runs continuously. It monitors all of our   interactions with others while updating our trust level for each person. When we interact with someone for the first time, we walk away with a measure of trust. Sometimes we might feel great—a high level of trust. Or we leave with the trust meter pegged at the bottom—a "slimy" feeling. If we know and understand what behavior elements go into creating trust, we can then make sure we deliver these behaviors to those we want to positively influence.

Elements of Trust

Two elements must be addressed in every interaction. First is the technical issue that's being dealt with. Second is the personal issue.

The **technical issue** is the subject that's being dealt with or talked about—the details, the issues. For example, when talking about a report the other person generated, the technical issue is the content, the conclusions, and who was involved in generating the data, etc.

The **personal issue** is the person's attachment to the subject. Attachment can be a plus or a minus, depending on past experiences, values, and beliefs. It comes from their personal frame of reference. In the business report example, it's the sum of the long hours they put into the report, the new insights it sparks, and their expertise. They have created a strong, positive attachment to this report.

For the other person's trust meter to be high, your response better be accurate on the technical issues and reflect empathy on their personal attachment to the report. Caution: A lot of issues in the work environment seem purely technical, but in reality, almost everyone brings a personal aspect that must not be ignored.

Deliver the Core Dimensions

Let's look at how we build trust. Psychologists have identified these four Core Dimensions of human nourishment: Respect, Empathy, Specificity, and Genuineness. All four are necessary to build a positive level of trust.

Respect: We all want respect, which has two aspects. First is acceptance, that is, we want to be accepted for who we are. We want to feel it's okay to be an individual and that we're not being judged and found wanting. The second aspect is feeling we have a right to our opinion. People don't have to agree with us, but it's important to show it's okay for us to think and feel the way we do. For example, if you communicate that you both accept us and our right to have an opinion, our trust meter for you goes up.

Empathy: We want to know people understand our thoughts and feelings and how we might have come to have them. Empathy means we can identify what the other person is thinking or feeling. More than that, we understand it because we've had similar thoughts or feelings.

We don't have to be experiencing it at the moment; we simply communicate our recognition and understanding of the other person's experience.

Dick's Rule: Share your wisdom, not your story.

Some people who are more Thinkers than Feelers have a difficult time showing empathy. If that describes you, a good response when others are telling you their thoughts and feelings is simply to respond with the word "Oh." Saying "Oh" shows you are paying attention and encourages the other person to continue talking. You can say "Oh" in many different ways, reflecting happy or sad feelings.

Also, saying "Oh" keeps you from stealing the spotlight by telling your similar story. I used to think doing that showed empathy, but I learned that it didn't. It's better to share what I learned from my similar experience without telling the whole story.

Specificity: The more specific we are in our communications, the higher the trust meter. Conversely, the more vague and general the communication, the lower the trust meter. Words in the conversation such as "you always" or "you never" tend to send the trust meter down. For example, consider the car salesman who says, "This car will last forever, and if it breaks down, we will fix it" versus the one who says, "This car has a 100,000-mile warranty on drive-train components but not tires and windshield wiper blades." The more specific you can be, the higher the trust you'll likely receive.

Genuineness: This fourth Core Dimension is determined from seeing people behave consistently over time. Are you the same in similar circumstances, behaving congruently? Do your words match your actions? If others say they are glad to see you, do they show it? When people believe you are genuine, the trust meter goes up. Conversely, if you are a phony, it goes down.

To increase trust in communications, deliver your message using the four Core Dimensions.

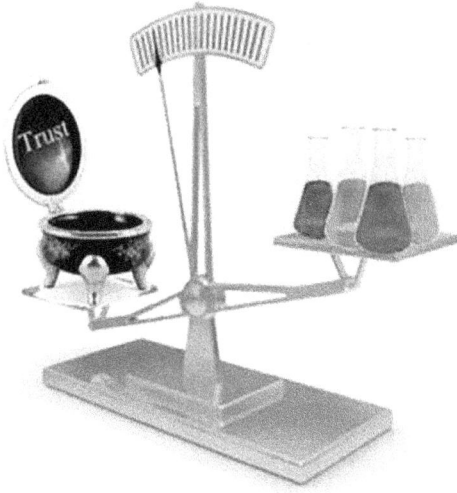

Maintain Trust Account

Trust is like a bank account; sometimes it's full and sometimes it's almost empty. We use up trust through our unthinking behaviors such as being judgmental or comments (e.g., "most of the items in the report were accurate") or devaluing others (e.g., "I'll look at the report you did if I need it."). Keeping an eye on trust requires work to maintain it at a high level. When we have a high level of trust, all of our interactions are easier and faster.

Questions Can Destroy Trust

It's true we need to ask questions to gain information and clarify points. We ask the Un-Ableness Question. People can ask questions that are manipulative and judgmental. My mentor Bob Weyant says that questions can be the "cow patties" in the pasture of life.

Questions Defined:

"In everyday conversation, a question is a poor substitute for more direct communications. Questions are incomplete, indirect, veiled, impersonal, and consequently ineffective messages that often breed defense reactions and resistance. They are rarely simple requests for information but an indirect means of attaining an end, a way of manipulating the person being questioned." – Jacques Lalanne

How we ask questions affects trust, especially if we forget to apply the Core Dimensions: Respect, Empathy, Specificity, and Genuineness. "Why did you do such a stupid thing?" is a trust-reducing question. Many times questions contain a hidden Behavior Request. For example, when your boss asks, "Are you busy right now?" you can be sure he or she has something in mind for you to do.

We call these trust-reducing questions **one-frame-of-reference** questions. They are one-frame because only the asker knows the frame of reference. The receiver has to guess the frame of reference, and this uncertainty lowers the trust meter.

The better approach is to use a **two-frame-of-reference** question, which builds trust because it provides the missing information. It gives both parties the frame of reference information. For example, the boss says, "We just got an urgent request from a customer. Are you busy right now?" That gives you the "because." It provides enough information for you to respond, and the trust meter goes up.

One-frame-of-reference questions can be okay if you have high trust. They are also okay if both parties have the same frame of reference, such as both working on a technical issue.

If you have any doubt about the other person understanding you or about the level of trust or about any unwillingness you sense, it's better to use the two–frame-of-reference question.

Change your questions

Changing how we ask questions is hard to do. We've had many years of training in the wrong way to use questions. But when you catch yourself asking a one-frame question, and get that questioning look in the other person's eyes like a "deer in the headlights," all you have to do is add "The Because."

When you get a one-frame question from someone, clarify it.

Don't guess: Ask for "The Because."

Be aware of hidden Behavior Requests

Typically, we have learned to ask questions rather than ask for action. We think it's more tactful or we don't want to have to deal with hearing "no." As a result, many questions contain a hidden Behavior Request. "You're not going to eat all of that cookie are you?" Clearly, it's not only a request for information; you want part of the cookie. Instead, request the behavior you want and say, "Please share your cookie with me"; don't hide it in a question.

Never ask "why?"

I know this seems like a contradiction because I said "Why?" is the code word for the Expressive Style, but let me explain. If you ask someone, "Why did you do or say that?" you open the door to problems.

First, it's a one-frame-of-reference question. The other person doesn't know why you are asking, so the trust meter goes down.

Second, it causes most people to put up their defenses. We learned growing up that when others asked that question, they weren't looking for information. It usually meant we were wrong and should have done or said something else—something they thought we should have said or done. But the initial reaction is to defend ourselves.

Third, if others are stuck in Victim Behavior and are asked "why," you'll hear reasons that go on for a long, boring time.

If you really want to know why, use a Two-Frame of Reference question.

You often want to know the thought process or background that led to a decision or action (e.g., "I'm not clear; could you give me the background for your decision or action?"). Another phrase to use is "Help me understand . . . ."

In the business world, the primary focus isn't why someone says or does something. Independent of their thoughts and feelings, we need them to say and do whatever moves the business forward. Focusing on the "right behavior" is more productive than spending time speculating on reason or motive.

Optimize Nonverbal Behaviors

Even when we're not talking, we are still communicating our thoughts and feelings. These nonverbal behaviors dramatically affect the trust meter. Humans are good at noticing slight changes in behavior such as a raised eyebrow, rolled eyes, or slumped posture. We hear voice changes in tone, pace of speech, and volume. We notice when someone is too much "in our space." What's worse, we attach meaning to these small movements.

Here are the things we notice:

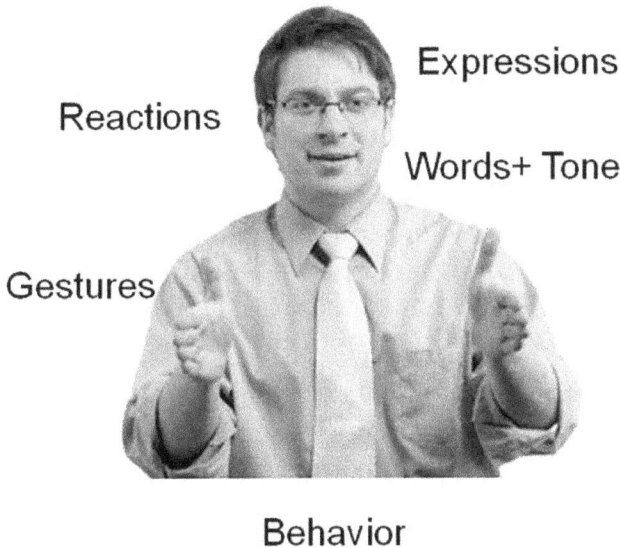

Expressions

Reactions

Words+ Tone

Gestures

Behavior

Remember:

It's your behavior *that influences others,*

not *your intentions or words.*

Problematically, we almost immediately judge what these small changes mean—and we do it subconsciously. For example, when a manager tells us about a new policy but he has slumped shoulders and a tired tone, he shows he doesn't believe in what he's saying.

"Shifty eyes can't be trusted" is another judgment. We make judgments like these about people all the time. We don't always realize that others are making the same judgments about us. Our signals are often perceived as a deficit of the Core Dimensions of Respect, Empathy, Specificity, and Genuineness, which lowers the trust meter.

Remember, the higher the trust meter, the more likely the outcome of the interaction will be positive.

Judgments Lower Trust

As noted earlier in this handbook, we more easily relate to people who have a SOCIAL STYLE similar to ours; therefore, we trust people who are most like us. By comparison, we're not sure about those people who are different from us and often attach negative adjectives to their behaviors.

When you interact with people you don't know, they are making judgments about you based only on your behaviors. Because in the business environment we can't choose whom we interact with based on SOCIAL STYLE, many times we start out with a trust deficit just because we are different from those we deal with.

If you behave only from your comfort zone—your home-base SOCIAL STYLE—the other person's trust meter for you will go down. The solution is simple and direct: Use the Platinum Rule and emulate that person's SOCIAL STYLE. When you do, you'll deliver the Core Dimensions, especially Empathy (making them feel more comfortable) and Respect (accepting them for who they are and that it's okay). You are also delivering Genuineness showing you care and are making an effort.

Key Nonverbal Trust Builders

It's important to use **eye contact** in an interaction for two reasons. First, for the speaker, it shows "Hey, I'm talking to you." Second, for the listener, it shows, "Hey, I'm listening."

"Tell-Assertive" friends prefer what I call strong eye contact. They believe that, if you aren't looking directly at them, you are disinterested, disrespectful, and inattentive. "Ask-Assertive" friends like and practice intermittent eye contact. Analytical style friends look at you when they're listening, look away when they're thinking, then look back again to listen. They are doing exactly what more Tell-Assertive friends want. They're thinking about what's being said.

Remember:

1. *Comfortable eye contact varies according to SOCIAL STYLE. Don't make judgments based on it.*

2. *You can modify your eye contact to build trust.*

Physical distance is something we notice only when someone is too close. So we normally move up to someone to a proximity point where we feel comfortable. Not everyone has the same "comfort" distance. When someone "invades" our space, it makes us uncomfortable and our trust meter goes down. I use arm's length as the unit of measurement. Amiable Style and Driving Style people are comfortable right at arm's length, while Analytical Style people feel comfortable at greater than arm's length. Meanwhile, Expressive Style friends like to be inside of arm's length.

What distance makes you uncomfortable? The point is that we unconsciously affect the trust meter. So to increase the trust, you would move to where the other person is comfortable.

Appropriate business touch. One SOCIAL STYLE is much more comfortable with touch than the other three. Yes, it's Expressive Style people. They like to stand inside arm's length so they can give you a pat on the shoulder, a hand on the arm, or an elbow nudge. This is great for other Expressive Style people, but doesn't work at all for the Analytical Style and the Driving Style. Amiable Style people have to have established a positive relationship before they feel comfortable. This requires being sensitive to the other person's comfort level: That's how to increase trust.

You never are invisible. In a meeting or group interaction, many people behave as if they think they are invisible. They believe if they aren't the one talking no one notices them.

Yet from experience being the one talking, we notice these "invisible" nonverbal messages from members of the group. These include a far-off stare, a quick check of phone messages, and a not-so-subtle look of disapproval. We assign meaning to these behaviors. Of course, we have no confirmation that we assigned the correct meaning. After all, the pained look on someone's face may have only been caused by a gas bubble.

If you want to maintain a high level of trust with the people in the group, pay attention to your nonverbal messages and body language. I especially recommend having appropriate attending behavior as a trust-builder. This includes:

1. "Square up" your posture while facing the speaker.

2. Make sure your eyes have their "lights on" to show you're listening and following the speaker.

3. Give appropriate nonverbal feedback that fits the speaker's Social Style.

Applications – Build the Trust

You want to build and maintain a high level of trust to be more effective in all of your interpersonal interactions. Sometimes you have to ask people to do things that are above and beyond the normal. In effect, these requests count as a withdrawal from the trust account. If the account is low to start with, you are in trouble. You also may consciously want to build up trust when you know you'll have to make a withdrawal in the near future. The following is specific advice for people in various job positions.

Manager / Supervisor

Maintaining a high level of trust with direct reports just makes sense. These are the people who support you, follow your lead, and produce results. If the trust level is high, the emergency quick-response situations are handled much faster than if trust is absent.

Sometimes you'll need to make advanced deposits in the trust account such as conducting a difficult performance review or asking someone for a significant change in behavior. The message is to make sure you keep an eye on the trust account of each employee.

Project Manager/ Team Lead

Keeping a high level of trust gives you another tool of persuasion. It creates the team environment that increases productivity and effectiveness. Plan on spending effort and time keeping the trust level high on the team.

Within the team, high trust is also important. Getting agreed-upon team behaviors built around the Core Dimensions sets the expectation for maintaining the trust environment.

Team member / Co-worker / Direct Report

You want your boss and co-workers to trust you, knowing life is easier in a high-trust environment. You can build that trust with the people you work with. Deliver the Core Dimensions and use two-frame-of-reference questions.

Help build the environment you can enjoy and thrive in.

Review

> ➤ Keep your trust account balance high.

> ➤ Deliver the Core Dimensions.

> ➤ Preserve trust with two-frame questions.

> ➤ Be aware of your nonverbal messages.

PERSUASION SKILLS

How do I persuade people to do what needs to be done?

How do I keep from creating conflict?

You have the Adaptation Skills to build rapport, influencing people to be more willing to work with you. Next, the Persuasion Skills come into play when asking for the specific desired behavior and handling either a "yes" or "no" response.

Confrontation is the first of the Persuasion Skills. Some of us hesitate to confront because we feel guilty asking someone to do something they should already know to do and/or because we fear conflict. Let's address both of those issues.

One definition of confrontation is simply to come front to front with someone, to "confront." Conflict is not a required part of the definition. Yet many of us have experienced face-to-face meetings getting out of hand and turning ugly.

How does conflict get added to the confrontation? What can we do to minimize its probability of happening?

Eliminate Causes of Conflict

Contributions to Conflict

Not Adapting to the Other's SOCIAL STYLE

Adaptation Skills enable us to take steps to make another person feel comfortable and trust us. When interacting, if we have not worked to adapt to the other person's SOCIAL STYLE, the probability of conflict increases. We see that conflict can come from these differences alone. We also see we can mistakenly convey the anti-Core Dimensions by being disrespectful, judgmental, vague, and phony. All of these significantly increase the chance of conflict—conflict that has nothing to do with the content of the interaction. It's all about how we present our information.

Bringing Our Emotional Baggage

Many times when we confront someone, we might bring our excess emotional baggage to the confrontation. If we are having a bad day (or bad life), we don't realize our negative feelings can seep into our confrontation. Consequently, we can take these feelings out on the other person.

Focusing on the Other's Wrong Behavior

We can focus on the other person's wrong behavior instead of what we want him or her to do right. Pointing out bad behavior makes people feel defensive, plus it takes away from focusing on what the desired behavior is.

Focusing on the Negative Consequences

When we dwell on the negative consequences of someone's behavior, what happens? Overemphasizing the negative may cause the person to argue about the validity of the consequences. If the person thinks exaggeration is at play, then we risk having our whole message discounted or ignored.

Blaming, Judging, and Making Inferences

We might use blame, and judge the other person's motives, but frankly, we can't know what goes on in another's mind. Remember, our inferences are usually not accurate and can make the other person feel defensive, thus escalating the conflict.

Defending the Need to Be Right

Being right is a way for us to feel good about ourselves, so we correct others, showing people how much we know that they don't know. We make assumptions and defend them as if they were truthful—all with the aim to show others they are wrong. And to what end?

I used to correct others all the time. What I've learned is that the accuracy of others' grammar or a second decimal point in a number is not important when they're expressing an idea, concept, or thought. Correcting their mistakes makes them feel defensive and me look bad.

My suggestion is to let go of your need to be right at the moment. If accuracy is important, come back later and address it.

New Definition

Use this definition of confrontation from now on:

Confrontation is coming face to face with a simple, respectful request for a specific behavior or a change in behavior.

Yes, you can make a respectful request of others; you have the right to ask. At the same time, realize that others always have the right to say "yes" or "no." And "no" is okay if they are willing to live with the consequences of that answer.

You will significantly increase your chances for a successful confrontation if you can:

1. Deliver a request using the Core Dimensions.

2. Be sensitive to the other person's SOCIAL STYLE.

3. Stay focused on the right desired behaviors and the positive consequences.

Confrontation Levels

If you get a "no" or a smoke screen, you can "up" your level of control and use a higher-level format. There are four levels of confrontation, allowing you to select the level most appropriate for the situation.

When you move up in levels, you are using up trust because the other person's degree of choice goes down.

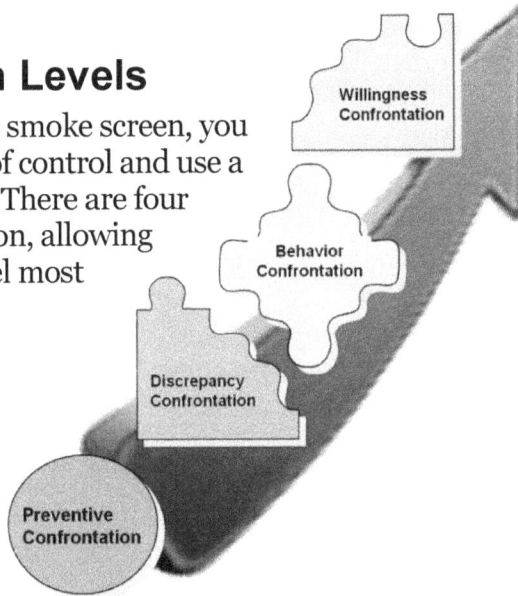

Willingness Confrontation

Behavior Confrontation

Discrepancy Confrontation

Preventive Confrontation

Do Preventive Confrontation

If an issue, opportunity, or required task comes up, you want to use Preventive Confrontation to create an Action Plan including the 4Ws: Who? What? When? Where?

This is good goal setting that's done early before any action is taken. You use this level at the initial point of determining what needs to be done. It could happen at the start of a project or when setting objectives for the coming period. It's when you decide who will do what.

Preventive confrontation is the key element to reduce your future hassles and misunderstandings. The goal is to clearly determine what you want as you share your visions, goals, priorities, expectations, and standards. Your job is to get the 4Ws.

This level of confrontation is considered the "best" form because of its low possibility of conflict. Done well, it sets clear expectations and garners early "buy-in" before something goes wrong. This level also allows people the most control over their actions and plans

Create the Behavior Request

At a later time, you may determine that performance expectations are not being met. That means you need to effect a behavior change, either returning to the original behavior or changing a specific behavior.

Here is the important part. You want to set this up so that if you start with the Discrepancy Confrontation and don't get a "yes," you can move up to the next confrontation level, the Behavior Confrontation level. If that doesn't work, you want to be able to move up to the Willingness Confrontation level. To do this, all the specific desired behaviors must be the same from one level to the other, so don't change them midstream.

Derive the Discrepancy and Willingness Request Formats

You would develop the Behavior Request first. The format contains three elements: degree of choice, specific behavior, and consequences. When you use this format, you increase the probability of getting a "yes" and reduce the probability of creating conflict—especially when you deliver it with the Adaptation Skills you've learned.

The Discrepancy Request is a "softer" version of Behavior Request. It's great to use when you don't have all the facts or information because it gives the other person the opportunity to explain what's going on in a nonthreatening way.

The Willingness Request is a "harder" version of the Behavior Request, used when you're getting resistance or continued nonperformance from the other person. With it, you are looking for accountability and commitment from that person.

Let's look at the format for the Behavior Request first.

Behavior Request Format

You confront someone to ask for a specific behavior or behavior change. Use this format for making that request. When you do, you will reduce the chance of conflict, increase the probability of success, and stay in control of the interaction.

[Name], I _____ to _____

          (degree of choice)   (specific right behavior)

And as a result _____

                  (describe the consequences)

Example:

"Sue, I (would like) you to (prepare the department resources distribution report by next Friday). As a result, (the department will be able to increase its efficiency—and you will be able to check that item off your personal objectives list)."

Tips for Writing a Behavior Request

Request Starts With "I"

You need to be the owner of the Behavior Request; you are the one who has used your Adaptation Skills to build rapport with the person involved.

Give Choices

The more choice you give someone, the higher the trust meter. Consider how much choice you're giving the other person. For example, you might say, "I would like you to consider . . ." This provides a high degree of choice. By comparison, saying, "I demand that you . . ." doesn't allow much choice at all.

Be Accurate

Be sure to say what you mean. Don't use "I'd like you to think about ," when you actually mean "I need you to . . ."

Specify Right Behaviors

This is the toughest part of this format. The more specific you are, the higher the probability you will get what you want. If you make a general request, you'll get an easy "yes" and the other person gets to decide what you meant. For example, if your request is "I want you to be more positive," the answer would be, "Sure, I'll be more positive." But you haven't said what, specifically, you want that person to do. So you come back a week later and say, "I don't see you being more positive." The person responds, "What do you mean? I quit calling everyone stupid."

To speak in more specific terms, you can include qualifiers such as "how much" and "by when." You can also describe the behavior by giving examples or explanations.

"For example, when we meet in the hall, please stop, acknowledge me, and say hello."

"By that I mean, when we're in a meeting with others, don't interrupt me when I'm speaking and don't call me a dummy in front of others."

Consequences That Motivate

People are motivated by consequences, which is the secret to getting the behavior you want.

Consequences can be positive or negative. People take action to gain positive consequences, or they take action to avoid negative consequences. Your job is to show them enough appropriate consequences so they take action on what you want. That will motivate them to say "yes" to your request.

Types of Consequences

Natural consequences flow without anyone's intervention. For example, you build your house next to the river and when the river

92

floods; your house is swept away. In business, you give good customer service and your customers come back.

Logical consequences flow logically. For example, if you meet the requirements for the position at a higher level, you get the promotion. If you miss work, you don't get paid.

Punitive consequences punish someone. For example, "I didn't like the format of your report, so you can't attend the management retreat." Don't use them because they lower the trust meter, and they make people defensive. Coercion elicits resistance.

Positive business consequences are good motivators (e.g., the project will be done on time).

Positive personal consequences are also good motivators (e.g., more vacation time, higher salary). Remember, the more personal the consequences, the more likely you'll get a "yes" to your request.

Negative consequences (e.g., taking away privileges) usually lowers the trust meter. So start with positive consequences. You can always add negative consequences later if needed.

In making a Behavior Request, avoid the following:

Fuzzy descriptions	E.g.: "You ignore company policy."
Character assassination	E.g.: "You behave like a big, insensitive jerk."
Creeping judgments	E.g.: "You waste company money on unnecessary items."
Inferences	E.g.: "You left the meeting because Frank criticized you."
Lengthy descriptions	E.g.: "You get involved with personal business and publish a poor quality report and miss important meetings . . ."
Profanity	Obviously, this brings down the trust level.

The Behavior Request must be clear, specific, and objective.

93

Discrepancy Request Format

We call this level of confrontation Discrepancy because there is a difference between what we are seeing and what we expected. So, we need to confront the individual to find out what's going on.

The beauty of this format is that we can maintain a high trust level when we don't know all the facts or reasons for the difference in performance.

I'm_____ because, on the one hand, you_____

  (genuine feeling/thoughts)   (expected right behavior)

while, on the other hand, you _____

                    (describe the undesirable behavior)

Example:

"Sue, I'm concerned because, on the one hand, your personal objective was to prepare the department resources distribution report by Friday, while, on the other hand, I haven't seen anything yet."

Discrepancy Confrontation Tips

Express Genuine Feeling or Thought
This is simply a statement of what you are thinking or feeling. (E.g., I'm confused, concerned, disappointed, frustrated, upset, etc.)

Note Expected Right Behaviors
This states what the others person agreed to do. It's also the same behavior you would use in the Behavior Request Format. It notes actions they agreed to do, commitments they promised, or statements they made. (You can work with the 4Ws.)

Sometimes, you need a behavior that you didn't have prior agreement on. The Expected Right Behaviors can be implied. They may derive from company values, team agreements, normally accepted standards, or professional expectations.

Describe Undesirable Behavior

Suppose you aren't getting the behavior you expected; either it's not happening or it's different from what you expected. Things need to change. Make sure your statement of their words, actions, or non-actions that you observed is descriptive, not judgmental. In effect, you're asking for clarification, while giving them a chance to explain before you jump to a conclusion.

The Discrepancy Confrontation is a powerful tool to use when you don't know all the facts: it's low risk. The investment may be that their answer starts a discussion and takes you to the Un-Ableness Question and 4Ws to get performance back on track. It works well in groups also.

The Discrepancy Format is a "soft" version of the Behavior Request format. Develop the Behavior Request first to make sure the expected right behavior is the same, and then adapt if needed.

Willingness Request Format

This is the top confrontation level. By the time you get to the point of using it, things have definitely not gone well. You haven't been getting clear answers and certainly haven't been getting the desired performance; that's why it seems abrupt.

With this format, we are only looking for commitment—only a simple "yes" or "no" that the person agrees to do what was asked.

I need to know if you are willing to _____. Yes, or no?

(specific right behavior)

Alternate Willingness Format

I need to know if you are willing to make a commitment right now to _____. Yes, or no?

(specific right behavior)

95

Willingness Confrontation Tips

Specific Right Behaviors
This must be the same right behavior that you used in the Behavior Request and the Discrepancy Request.

Translate the Response
Most of time, you won't hear a simple "yes" or "no" answer. Instead, you'll get a story, a smoke screen, or some kind of resistance. Do not get drawn into a discussion or an argument. Remember, you're only looking for a "yes" or "no" response. You might use the phrase, "I assume your response is a 'no' at the moment."

> **Key Goal:**
>
> *Accountability: No matter what the response, translate it into a "yes" or a "no."*

Act on the Response
For a "yes" response, reaffirm or renegotiate the 4Ws to build a solid action plan.

For a "no" response, you can either accept it and deliver the consequences or use the No Strategies presented in the Clarifying the Response section later in this handbook.

Create a Positive Experience

The conflict in confrontation arises not so much from the behavior you are asking for but from the way the request is delivered. When you are confronting people using this new Behavior Request approach, they may be confused and become defensive because it's different than what they know. The following tips will help.

Tips for Creating a Positive Experience

Ask for Forgiveness

Because people remember past experiences and you may have done confrontation poorly in the past, perhaps it's time to reset the stage and clarify what's going on. I call it "asking for forgiveness first."

First, say you're sorry for creating any past misunderstandings or doing a poor job of communicating. Then explain you've learned a new approach that works well, and you'd like to try it in this situation.

Anticipate the Response

Asking for a behavior change is usually not a surprise to most people. It's more important to remember that they don't like to be reminded of "bad" behavior. It's not comfortable for them, and it tends to make them feel defensive and angry.

When you ask for positive behavior, one third of the people know they need to change. They'll voluntarily admit to the wrong behavior and agree to correct it. You likely don't have to bring up the "bad" behavior at all.

The second third of the people know they need to change and will gladly agree to the new behavior when you ask for positive behavior. They are relieved and thankful that you didn't bring up the "bad" behavior.

The final third category of people will deny they need to change. They'll get defensive and argue with you. For these people, be sure to have two examples of the "bad" behavior. If you have none, then it becomes your opinion against theirs. But having two examples makes it hard to refute the "bad" behavior.

Deliver the Request in a Positive Way

How you deliver the Behavior Request makes all the difference. As all these tips emphasize, you should be focused on the right behavior and positive consequences as you deliver it with the Core Dimensions in mind.

Never make it a "hit and run" confrontation. Rather, it's the start of a process of interacting with the other person. If you initially get a "yes" response, then get the 4Ws next. If you received a "no," then apply the No Strategies discussed in an upcoming section.

Plan the Confrontation Process

Sometimes a pending confrontation can be risky, especially if it's a situation you have strong feelings about or the other person is likely to react emotionally. It could even be a situation in which you feel vulnerable or one with a risk of retaliation or physical harm.

In all of these situations, planning in detail will make the confrontation less risky and easier to accomplish. By planning thoroughly, you'll be in control of the confrontation process.

Prepare Well

As you prepare, you want to do the following: Review the person's SOCIAL STYLE and adapt your confrontation to that style. If, for example, the person is of the Amiable Style, plan to spend time nurturing the relationship before making the Behavior Request.

Build trust ahead of time if possible.

Decide to deliver all the Core Dimensions during the confrontation.

Review this checklist carefully in case any is deemed a show stopper. Each is explained following the list.

Confrontation Check List

- *What do you want?*
- *Is it worth it?*
- *How far will you go?*
- *Is it appropriate?*
- *WPPSS?*
- *Examples?*
- *What level to start?*

- *Need context?*
- *Expected "no"?*
- *Handle emotions?*
- *How much time?*
- *What's the next level?*
- *Right person 1st?*
- *Ducks in line?*

What do you want? This is the key question. What, specifically, do you want from the other person? The lower your specificity; the higher your chance of conflict.

Is it worth it? Sometimes it's best to just let things go and get on with your life. This is especially true if you are confronting to defend your need to be right. For example, I may like to use a priority system of A, 1, 2, 3; B, 1, 2, 3; whereas my colleague may like a Top 10 priority list. Should I confront him about that? No, it's not worth it.

How far will you go? Are you willing and able to deliver the consequences implied in your Behavior Request?

Is it appropriate? Should you do the confrontation? For example, should you confront the employee of another manager, or should that manager do it?

WPPSS? What is the Worst Possible, Probable, Scary Scenario— that is, what's the worst thing that could happen? What's the probability of that happening? And if it does happen, can you live with it?

Examples? Do you have two specific examples of the behavior you want changed? (It's much easier for the other person to argue with you if you only have one example.) Don't use them unless you have to when making the Behavior Request because two thirds of the people will know they need to make a behavior change and don't need to be taken through the "bad" behavior.

What level of confrontation? Choose the level of behavior request that is appropriate for the situation.

Need context? Sometimes people can feel uncomfortable or threatened when you confront them. You can reduce that probability by putting this confrontation into a larger context. For example, you might say, "Sue, you are a valuable member of our team. I enjoy our working relationship. And I need to ask you to... (state your Behavior Request).

Expected "no" response? Sometimes people become upset when confronted, reacting differently than you might expect depending on their SOCIAL STYLE. Review the upcoming section on Reactive No's and be prepared to handle unexpected responses.

Handle emotions? Anticipate the other person's emotional response and prepare to handle any anger, crying, silence, and so on that comes up.

How much time? Remember that this confrontation is the beginning of a conversation. You will end up with the 4Ws and may uncover a more urgent issue that needs to be dealt with first. Always plan to give this process enough time; don't hurry it.

What's the next level? Be prepared to move up to the next level of confrontation if you get resistance or a smoke screen in response.

Right person first? Sometimes you need to talk to someone else before the confrontation. For example, if you are confronting a peer, you may need to alert your supervisor that you're working on an issue and need support. According to the new definition of confrontation, alerting your supervisor is considered another confrontation, so use as much of the Confrontation Process as you need and make sure to get the 4Ws.

Do you have your follow-up steps lined up? Depending on the outcome of the confrontation, several actions may have to happen in sequence. Make sure all steps are set up to happen if need be.

> **Do your homework to be in control of the situation.**

Set the Stage for a Successful Confrontation

Have enough time and select a private place

Make sure you have plenty of time and pick a place with privacy where you feel safe. You may need to have another person present, perhaps from human resources. In extreme situations, you may need to have company security ready to come in.

Enter into the discussion with good faith

Your goal is to help others gain the natural positive consequences of their behavior change. Putting forth your best effort is necessary for positive results. Remember:

1. Deliver all of the Core Dimensions.

2. Respect all parties involved.

3. Express appreciation for the other person's participation and effort.

4. Look only for a "yes" or "no" answer to your Behavior Request, nothing more.

5. With a "yes" answer, follow up with the 4Ws.

6. With a "no" answer, apply the No Strategies in the following section.

**If you sense any threat of physical harm,
DON'T CONFRONT.**

Applications – Confront without Conflict

Confrontation usually happens one on one. It's not reserved only for "bad" things. It can be initiated by anyone at any level. That's why our definition is simply to come face to face with the other person.

The key to successful interactions is to confront early in a situation before things get out of control. The Discrepancy format is extremely useful when you are not sure what's going on. Simply use it for clarification.

Here's how anyone can apply this confrontation tool.

Manager / Supervisor

The Behavior Request format is very effective with direct reports. It gives you an arsenal to use at different times in different circumstances. The planning checklist is an important tool when you have to confront someone in a difficult situation. Remember to couch your Behavior Request with all of the Adaptation Skills described. The higher the trust and the more you adapt to the person's SOCIAL STYLE, the better your chances of getting a "yes." Remember, even though you have position power, using it depletes your trust account.

Project Manager / Team Lead

The Discrepancy format and the Behavior Request should be among your everyday tools. They are designed to avoid creating conflict and deliver the Core Dimensions while getting results. Realize that much of the conflict comes from how the request is delivered, not

what you ask for. Review known sources of conflict to avoid them. Invest in the Adaptation Skills to increase your effectiveness. Describe enough relevant consequences (something to gain or avoid) to motivate your team.

Team Member / Co-worker / Direct Report

The Behavior Request is a powerful tool for you to use in all of your team interactions. To increase your success rate, determine the levels of Behavior Requests to provide additional options.

102

If you report to someone, the Discrepancy Format is a great way to interact with your boss. It allows you to confront in a positive, respectful way. The main limitation is the degree of choice you can give the other person. Making demands of your boss may not be an option, but you will more likely succeed by stating solid, positive business consequences.

Review

> Leave your emotional baggage out of any confrontation.

> Regard the confrontation as a simple request for a behavior change.

> Use the Behavior Request format to help you link behavior to consequences.

> Plan in detail when facing risky situations

Am I getting a clear "yes" or a clear "no"?

Human beings communicate a lot. But many times it feels as if we are communicating in a fog. Clarity does not come naturally to the process. And as we have seen, much of the conflict we have to deal with comes from lack of clarity and lack of specificity.

Let's look at what we can do to clear things up and develop strategies for dealing with the lack of clarity and specificity from others.

Send Clear Messages

Clearer messages get clearer responses.

One thing we are in charge of is the messages we put out. The clearer the message we send, the clearer the response we get back.

Specificity is key to success.

Specificity also raises the trust level. Remember, the Trust Meter is based on two components. One is the technical issue being discussed—the "It." The other is the feelings and thoughts attached to that issue—the "Attachment." Both need to be included in the communication.

To send a clear message, give "The Because."

As discussed in the section on asking good questions, to preserve your level of trust, you can use the Two-Frame-of-Reference question. That way, not only will you maintain the trust level by giving your frame of reference ("The Because"), you will clarify the message.

When you do this, the payoff can be significant. With a clear message, you can better understand the other person. This leads to better solutions and approaches, and you will get the desired action to happen sooner.

Give "I" Messages

Many of us never learned to clearly communicate. Rather, we learned things such as people tell "little white lies," "there is no I in team," and people have hidden agendas. As a result, we learned to camouflage our own feelings and positions so we didn't end up looking bad. We also used questions instead of stating our own thoughts and feelings. Remember this hidden Behavior Request: "You're not going to eat all of that cookie, are you?"

The point is that "I" messages are okay when delivered with empathy. They clarify your communications by providing information on your frame of reference. The format is to state the word "I" followed by what you think or feel in detail.

There is also an interesting phenomenon in which you get a response similar to the one you put out, as this example shows.

You talk about "It"; they talk about "It."

You talk about "Attachment"; they talk about "Attachment."

So if you want to know what people are thinking or feeling about "It" (their Attachment), you can talk about your thoughts and feelings and they will respond with their own thoughts and feelings.

When you give and receive "I" messages, they legitimize your frame of reference. In addition, they deliver the Core Dimensions of genuineness, help build trust, and achieve clear communications.

All you can be is you.

Be honest, open, and direct.

Accept the consequences of communicating this way.

Beware of Easy "Yeses"

Easy "yeses" often turn into "no's" later. It's because people will say "yes" even though they haven't thought through all the steps. Or they give an ambiguous answer that has some "no" in it. For example:

"Yes, I'll do it, God willing" = maybe 5 percent "no."

"Yes, I'll give it my best shot" = 50 percent "no."

"Absolutely not" = 100 percent "no."

Use the 4Ws to clarify the "yes" into something you can count on.

A rule of thumb:

Anything other than a clear "yes" is a "no" at the moment.

Reasons for "No"

People say "no" for one of two reasons: They're either unable or unwilling. It's important to uncover which one applies because you'd handle each one differently.

Unable

A person may be unable for many possible reasons. If you can help them become able, they can say "yes" to your Behavior Request. Consider these:

1. Person doesn't know what needs to be done. – Ask the Un-Ableness Question.

2. Person doesn't know how to do it. – Use training.

3. Person doesn't have enough/right resources. – Provide them.

4. Person has priorities set wrong. – Help reprioritize.

Identifying what people are unable to do is critical for developing their talents. When you can help increase their abilities and talents, it becomes a win for both parties.

Unable to become able

Sometimes a person is unable to become able. Realize the difference between ability and ableness. Ableness is visible—something a person can do now. Ability is an inside job, a person's potential.

Many people have the ability to become able, but the main question is this: Can they do what you need now? You want to make specific assignments based on Ableness.

> **Ableness Test**
>
> **Have I ever seen the person do what I want (or something similar) at the level I need them to do it?**

If you haven't seen them do a similar behavior then do not give them the responsibility.

Unwilling

People say "no" because they may believe they have too much on their to-do list already. They may be hesitant or afraid because they're out of practice or not sure of their ability to be successful, and sometimes they simply don't want to.

Three Types of Unwilling "No"

Clear "No"

In this case, you can use the 10 No Strategies to change this type of "no" to a "yes." (See the following section on Strategies for Handling the Clear "No.")

Hidden "No"

The "no" is usually hidden in a smoke screen. People use a lot of words but not all of them is "yes" or "no." You would first cut through the smoke screen to get a clear "no" and then use the No Strategies techniques. (See the following section on Strategies for Handling Smoke Screens.)

Reactive "No"

This refers to a strong emotional response when the Behavior Request accidentally pushes the other person's button. The person doesn't say "yes" or "no"; instead, he or she blows up. At this point, most people quickly "fold their tent" and get out, but you don't have to do that. (See Strategies for Handling the Reactive "No.")

"No" Can Be Okay

All of the tools presented to this point are designed to significantly increase the probability of you getting a "yes" to your Behavior Request. If that hasn't happened yet, here are 10 additional tools to use. But first of all, know that saying "no" can be okay.

- "No" is okay if the person gives a valid business reason and stays open to negotiation (e.g., *"I can't help you because I have this task to complete. If you help me do the task, I can help you on your request."*).

- It's okay if the person says "no," provides no input, and gives up control (e.g., *"No, I can't provide the input, and I will accept whatever you decide."*).

Strategies for Handling a Clear "No"

These strategies come under four categories: Clarification Strategy, Walk Away Strategies, Personal Power Strategies, and Position Power Strategies.

Clarification Strategy

This is the first strategy because you need to verify that you, in fact, did get a "no." Remember learning about how people don't say "no" clearly? They might react or go silent. This clarification strategy uses the following phrase:

I assume your response is a "no" at the moment, right?

Get verification or clarification. Many times a person is just venting and really means to say "Yes."

Walk Away Strategies

Accept the "no" and walk away. Sometimes it's not worth the additional effort to convert the "no" to a "yes."

Do it yourself. Accept the "no," walk away, and do it yourself. Sometimes this is the easiest option.

Get someone else to do it. Accept the person's "no" and find someone else to do it.

Wait and try again. Sometimes people are unable to say "yes" to your request at the moment. But if they accomplish their current tasks, they may be able later to take on the task you are requesting.

Personal Power Strategies

Negotiate. Look for a win/win solution. Is there something you can do for them or resources you can provide that will enable them to work on your task?

Change degree of choice. Increase the level of urgency in your Behavior Request. Sometimes people don't realize the importance of a task.

Add more consequences. Remember, the consequences you included in your Behavior Request are what motivate the person to say "yes." To emphasize them, you can restate your request adding additional business consequences. Make sure you have included personal consequences that are important to the other person. You can add the negative consequences of what will happen if they say "no." And you want to confirm that others understand the consequences and are willing to live with them.

Before leaving the personal power strategies, ask the following question:

> **Is there anything I can say or do to change your "no" to a "yes"?**

This is an important question because many times people will tell you what they need and many times you can provide it. For example, the person says, "If someone would just help me finish the task I'm on, I could do yours." If it's something you could do yourself or get resources to help you do, you have turned the "no" into "yes."

Position Power Strategies

If you have position power, now is the time to use it. It's not earlier on the list because when you use position power, it reduces the trust level. But if you have tried all the trust-preserving strategies to no avail, you need a "yes" now.

Get a higher authority. This is the last resort, but it's also how business is structured. At times you have to go up the chain of command. If you do, always let the other person know this is your next step. Ask to see if he or she would prefer to handle it between the two of you.

Final Shot

If, after you've used the skills and strategies you have learned, you still end up with a "no" (it can happen), here's one final statement you could make. You could say,

> *"I'll accept the 'no'; however, you give me no choice but to go ahead alone. I will therefore assume you support my actions."*

This statement is a key to clarifying the person's support or opposition. You hope he or she gives you a response that your results will be supported. However, it's good to know early if that person will fight you on what you are doing. It gives you a head start on handling the "cow patties."

Handling Smoke Screens

Many times, people respond to your request with a smoke screen, which is when you can't easily tell if they are saying "yes" or "no." In fact, it's usually so smoky that you're not sure if they even gave you an answer to your question.

Smoke screens are not often put up on purpose. You have likely learned ways to respond to requests that minimize your risks and hassles. Plus people unconsciously avoid taking on more tasks or assignments. They make sure what they're being asked to do is more important or more urgent than the already long list of things they're working on.

The smoke screen from the other person can distract you enough that you leave without getting an answer to your Behavior Request. That person still didn't have to give you a "no."

Examples:

Don't get hooked on these classic smoke screens:

- ☐ **Changing the subject.** You make your Behavior Request and the other person changes the subject: e.g., a recent sports event, the weather, today's gossip, the reorganization. You discuss the new subject or series of subjects and enjoy a great conversation, but you end up without an answer. Many times, people change the subject to how overloaded and overworked they are, so you decide not to pursue it any longer. They didn't say "no"; in effect, you "folded your tent" and left.

- ☐ **Questioning.** This is a difficult smoke screen because often the questions are legitimate. Some questions may need to be answered, but many are not directly related to whether the person can do what you asked. You try to answer all the questions, but eventually they come up with one you can't answer. Rather than pin down if they will do it, you "fold your tent" and go away promise to resume you get an answer.

- ☐ **Being technically dazzling.** This happens when the person you ask knows a lot more about a subject than you do. Rather than say "no," the person goes off on all the technical problems he or she can imagine. You are not as familiar with the subject, so you can't argue. Finally, you decide to withdraw your request. The person didn't say "no"; you assumed it.

- ☐ **Venting.** Some people use Venting as a smoke screen. Whenever you make a request, they whine, moan, and groan enough that you finally "fold your tent" and go away. They never give you a clear "yes" or "no."

- ☐ **Others**. Others can be highly creative. Or, some smoke screens can be as simple as "I have to talk to my boss" or "I'll have to get back to you."

How Smoke Screens Work

The smoke screen works because you get hooked into a conversation that drifts away from your intended purpose—i.e., to get an answer to a Behavior Request. And people seem to know which smoke screen hooks you; what your favorite subject is or your level of technology. They know what engages you.

Again, I don't believe most people consciously manipulate others with smoke screens. Rather, it's an unconscious, evolutionary process. They've learned what has worked in the past, so they adapt their smoke screens to new situations, believing the tactic will work for them in the future.

So what can you do to cut through others' smoke screens?

Cutting Through the Smoke

The way to handle each of the different smoke screens is the same.

- Stay engaged with the conversation but don't get hooked on the smoke.

- Identify legitimate concerns and table them for later discussion. Say, "That's a good question, we'll come back to it."

- Refocus the person on the Behavior Request, looking for only a "yes" or "no" answer. Say, ". . . what I need to know from you is . . ." and make a Behavior Request.

- Say, "That's not the issue."

- Or say, "Let me refocus . . . ."

- Give short, quick, respectful responses and move on:

"Yes, I saw the game. It was great because . . . ."

"Yes, I agree with that . . . ."

"No, that's not true . . . ."

"Sorry to hear that . . . ."

Handle the "yes" with the 4Ws.

Anything other than a clear "yes" is a "no" at the moment.

113

Handling the Reactive "No"

When people's stress increases, their reaction can be predicted based on their SOCIAL STYLE. Specifically, it's based on their Assertiveness, Responsiveness, and one other characteristic called Pace.

Pace is tied directly to Assertiveness and describes how quickly that STYLE responds. The higher the Assertiveness, the quicker the response, almost to the point of startling the people around you.

STYLE	ASSERTIVENESS	RESPONSIVENESS	PACE	RESPONSE
EXPRESSIVE	High	High	Fast	**Attack**
AMIABLE	Low	High	Slow	**Acquiesce**
ANALYTICAL	Low	Low	Slow	**Avoid**
DRIVING	High	Low	Fast	**Autocratic**

What to Do

To use a metaphor about sailing in a small boat in tropical waters, occasionally a small, windy rainstorm or squall will engulf you—a reactive "no." These squalls come up suddenly and leave just as suddenly. You drop anchor and hold on so you don't get blown away. You wait a few minutes for it to dissipate, and then you get back to sailing.

Let's look at how to handle each style's reactive "No."

Expressive Style

When a Behavior Request accidently pushes these people's buttons, they get angry. They suddenly attack verbally and often attack you personally.

Their anger is like a squall. It needs wind to sustain it. Without the fierce winds, the squall dissipates quickly. Here's what you do:

1. Provide no wind to fuel the anger. (Keep quiet. Almost anything you say may be perceived as "wind.")

2. Wait for 30 seconds to a minute. (Reactive anger will dissipate quickly, although a smoke screen may not.)

114

3. Acknowledge that you notice their strong feelings. (These are Feeling people who just dumped a bucket of feelings in front of you. If you don't acknowledge their feelings, you provide more wind for the squall.)

4. Refocus them on your Behavior Request. (You may need to set up another meeting to deal with the cause of the anger.)

5. Determine their "yes" or "no" response.

Amiable Style

People with this SOCIAL STYLE are relationship-oriented and, when pushed, they will acquiesce; they say "yes" to end the discomfort. Be alert that they may not follow through: they will get even.

This SOCIAL STYLE reflects emoting—most of them cry—but without the assertiveness. Most people don't like to deal with that response. So try the same approach as used for anger.

1. Don't provide any wind to fuel the squall.

2. Wait 30 seconds to a minute. (The tears take longer to dissipate than anger, and Amiable style people tend to carry on a conversation while regaining control.)

3. Since they are Feeling people, be sure to acknowledge that you noticed and understand their feelings.

4. Then refocus them on your Behavior Request.

5. Determine their "yes" or "no" response.

Analytical Style

The people in this SOCIAL STYLE are neither emotive nor assertive. Rather, their reactive response is to avoid. These people walk out – or worse – they shut down right in front of you and refuse to communicate. This is the hardest group to get re-engaged. Try these suggestions:

1. Don't wait; it doesn't help, other than give them a minute to think.

2. Don't acknowledge their feelings; they don't relate to that approach and likely aren't displaying any.

3. Find a way to re-engage them. For example, ask them to help you understand what you said that was incorrect or off track. Their desire to get things right may re-engage them.

4. Refocus them on your Behavior Request.

5. Determine their "yes" or "no" response.

Driving Style

This SOCIAL STYLE is controlling, e.g., non-emotive and assertive. When they get their buttons pushed, they become autocratic. They talk louder and more forcefully to pressure you to understand better. What can you do? Hang in there and refocus them.

1. Waiting doesn't help.

2. There is no need to acknowledge feelings.

3. Get their attention by speaking equally forcefully. A phrase that seems to work: "That's not the issue." Because they are task-oriented and want it to be the right task, they'll say, "Well then, what is the issue?"

4. Now, refocus them on your Behavior Request.

5. Determine their "yes" or "no" response.

These exaggerated reactions may make you uncomfortable. You may leave or send the other person away to get his or her act together. You face two problems with this approach.

1. The Problem-Solving Process stops, so you don't make progress.

2. When you meet again, the same thing can happen.

Remember, you are making a respectful Behavior Request. All you want is a "yes" or a "no" response. So drop anchor, ride out the squall, refocus, and get your "yes" or "no."

The Confrontation Checklist asked what type of "no" you expect. These are your choices. If you know what to expect when people get their buttons pushed, you can plan to deal with their response putting you in control of the confrontation.

Applications – Clarification Skills

Your Clarification Skills can be used in all application areas. They are most effective when there is interaction between the parties, and information is exchanged. They work face to face, voice to voice, and screen to screen.

Manager / Supervisor

These Clarification Skills help managers get buy-in and commitment from their direct reports. At times, an employee is unable to do what is requested. Here, the manager may be able to help the person become able. Being unable may be due to a lack of resources or training, or it may be a conflict in priorities. By viewing confrontation as the start of a dialogue, you can work quickly to find optimum solutions.

Project Manager / Team Lead

Too many times, people get wrapped up in the day-to-day activities and are not clear what to do within their teams. These Clarification Skills let you clear up the smoke screen and any ambiguity so everyone can see the best course of action. The negotiation strategies are most useful with team members.

Team Member / Co-worker / Direct Report

All of the Clarification Skills are useful from this position. The only "no" strategy that doesn't work with the boss is position power. All the others can be an effective way to get more results and create a better working environment.

Review

- ➢ Send clear messages to get clear responses.
- ➢ Blow away the smoke and cut through to the "yes" or "no."
- ➢ Use the No Strategies to increase your "yeses."
- ➢ Be prepared for a reactive "no."

How do I make "yes" easier in future interactions?

Throughout this handbook, the focus has been to adapt to other people's SOCIAL STYLE, which helps you to persuade them to do the required behaviors. The critical leverage comes when you can get them to repeat the desired behaviors without going through the whole process again. This powerful skill is Positive Feedback.

The Power of Positive Feedback

Why We *Don't* Give Positive Feedback

First, most of us hesitate to give feedback because it causes us to expose our thoughts, feelings, and emotions. That makes us feel vulnerable.

Second, it takes time and work to be specific in our feedback. Also, if we make a mistake in citing the detail, we can look foolish. So we don't give effective feedback.

Why We *Should* Give Positive Feedback

First, it makes the other person feel good. Sadly, most of us believe we don't get enough positive feedback.

Second, when it's done right, it increases the trust level.

Third, it makes us feel good to give it.

The classic management mantra is, "Catch them doing something right and reward them." It's true. Behaviors that are rewarded get repeated. So the business reason to give positive feedback is to encourage more of the right behavior in the group.

Give Positive Feedback to get continued "right" behaviors.

120

Say Thank You

Sometimes, simple things are the most powerful. Similarly, the most overlooked words can have a dramatic, positive effect. When someone follows through on a Behavior Request you made, the organization benefits, the team benefits, and the individual benefits. What is the key to get ongoing right behaviors and continued positive support? Simply say, "Thank you."

When you get the behaviors you asked for, say "Thank you."

Use Effective Positive Feedback

Giving good positive feedback is not easy. Most experiences we have with it leave a bad taste in our mouths because it usually appears insincere or manipulative. Let's examine why it usually doesn't work and then determine how to make it effective.

Why It Hasn't Worked

Typical positive feedback—or compliments, as a lot of people think—don't work. In fact, they don't deliver the Core Dimensions, and they end up reducing trust. As a result, they don't reinforce positive behaviors. For example: "Hey, Don, you're looking sharp today." "I just wanted to compliment the work you did last week." "You'll go far in this company."*(I think these are three separate "compliments"; quotation marks needed.)*

Lacking Empathy

When people give feedback to you about you, then it's a "you" message and not an "I" message. You feel uncomfortable because you don't know where their comments are coming from. It's like the one-frame-of-reference question; it doesn't give any insight into what they are up to, your trust meter goes down.

Lacking Specificity

Most attempts at positive feedback are too general. If I said, "Jim, that was a great job last week," then Jim is thinking, I did a lot of things last week and all of them weren't so good. What specifically was great? Or if you say, "Mary, you're learning to be a great salesperson," Mary thinks, I still have a lot to learn. What, specifically, did I do well? Because there's no detail in your comments, the trust meter goes down.

Lacking Genuineness

Giving a compliment such as "Great shirt" or "You really stood up for yourself well today" is not considered specific positive feedback. In fact, when you receive a vague compliment yourself, your immediate response might be suspicion, embarrassment, or distrust. You wonder, What does that person want from me? Realize the trust meter goes down if you suspect you're about to be manipulated.

Positive Feedback That Works

As you have likely figured out by now, there is a format that can yield effective results.

I'm _____ because you _____.

   (genuine feeling/thought)   (describe specific right behavior)

And as a result _____.

         (describe positive consequences of the behavior)

Example:

I'm elated because you included the color graph in your report, and as a result, Mr. King could quickly see the profit margins. That significantly reduced the time it took him to make the decision.

You can see this is like the other formats in this handbook; it has an "I" message with thoughts/feelings that link to the specific right behaviors. The secret to success is making sure to include the positive consequences of people's behavior.

Most people don't know how to receive positive feedback. They usually discount it, claiming it wasn't really their doing or they don't deserve it. Be sure you get them to accept the feedback and make the link in their brain that their behavior got those good results. When they make that link internally, you will continue to get those right behaviors in the future. You may have to resort to your No Strategies to get them to accept it.

The only right response to positive feedback is THANK YOU.

Deliver Using the Core Dimensions

How you deliver feedback is important. The best way is face to face and in person with no barriers between you such as a desk or a table. In your delivery, you want to use all you've learned about emulating the person's SOCIAL STYLE. Also, remember to watch your nonverbal communications.

Be sure to include the Core Dimensions: Respect, Empathy, Specificity, and Genuineness. This format works well in both voice-to-voice and screen-to-screen communications; it also works with groups.

Give Public Recognition

Remember, we said that the business reason to give positive feedback is to encourage more of the right behavior in the group. This applies to any group, team, or committee you're involved with. If you are giving positive feedback to one of the members and you would like to reinforce that behavior in the rest of the group, deliver the feedback in public (i.e., in front of the group). You want people to make that mental link between right behaviors and positive results.

Sometimes people are shy and may be embarrassed if recognized in front of the group. There are two ways around that:

If you've done your homework well, all you're doing is pointing out something they did and showing the positive consequences of their actions. You're not falsely praising them. After all, they did the behavior.

Or, you can confront the person in private. Give positive feedback and then make a Behavior Request for permission for you to repeat the feedback in front of the group. Your higher goal is to reinforce right behaviors among those in the group.

Make a personal commitment to give one positive feedback per week or—better yet—one per day to people you interact with. Not only will you raise the trust level and make people feel better, but they will likely repeat the good behaviors in the future. This will make your world a better place.

Ask to Get Positive Feedback

What should you do if you think you don't get enough positive feedback? Obviously, with your new Confrontation Skills, you know how to simply ask for it without causing conflict or feeling guilty. Use the Discrepancy format or the Behavior Request format. After all, your needs are important, too.

By the way, if the person has no positive feedback for you, you need to know that. It may be time to consider your Three Choices. So be sure to ask.

If you don't get positive feedback, ask for it.

Applications – Positive Feedback

Positive feedback is great for everyone. Because your goal in using it is to get ongoing right behaviors, use it with everyone.

Team member / Co-worker / Direct Report

Give positive feedback to your team members, co-workers, and your boss This is a terrific way to interact with your boss or bosses. It gives you a structured way to reinforce her or his positive behaviors. For example, "Debra, I felt really empowered today when you let me run the meeting with our borrowed resource providers. As a result, I can be more effective in getting their buy-in and support on future projects."

Manager / Supervisor

As a manager, you can use positive feedback with all of your direct reports. It gives you an arsenal of options to use at different times in different circumstances. For example, in an email to an individual copied to the team, you'd say: "Naomi, I'm so pleased you came in on Sunday to reboot the server. As a result, the whole team can hit the ground running on Monday and keep us on schedule. Thank you."

Project Manager/ Team Lead

For team leaders, positive feedback is a perfect way to praise the team and increase commitment and morale. For example, "Team, I'm so impressed and proud. When the new CIO surprised us all with the 'new direction,' we certainly vented about it. But then we quickly focused on what we were able to do and came up with a modified strategy. We were the first group to produce a revised plan. Now, she considers us one of her top go-to teams for action and results. Well done."

Review

> The goal is to encourage the right behaviors to continue.

> Say thank you.

> Give effective positive feedback.

Making It All Work

Okay, what do I do next?

When will I get good?

You have been exposed to a number of People Skills in this handbook. As with any skills, you have to practice them to master them. When learning new skills, we go through four phases:

- Phase One is the knowledge phase. You learn about the skills and try them out.

- Phase Two is recognition. You become aware of situations in which you could apply the skills. Usually after the fact (e.g., "Oh gee, I could have used this skill in that situation.").

- Phase Three is application. You consciously practice the skills to get more comfortable with them.

- Phase Four is implementation. You actually implement the skills on a routine basis. The approaches, structures, and formats are second nature to you. You use them naturally.

Some situations that may fluster you and cause you to lose your anchor; that's to be expected. The saving grace of interacting with other people is that most of the time you can repair and improve any of your encounters. Be assured that none of the skills in this book will make your interactions worse.

Dick's Behavior Request to YOU:

I would like you to commit to start developing these skills immediately and, as a result, you'll take more control of your interactions and be more effective at work and more successful in your important relationships. You'll also demonstrate to others that change and growth are not only possible but profitable.

Following are suggestions to help you become more effective.

How do I master the concepts?

According to my colleagues Pamela J. Gordon and Tom Dearth, if you use a new skill seven times in 21 days, you own it. So create a Success Journal to plan and capture your successes. This helps you speed up the mastery process and provides a tool for reviewing, planning, and documenting your growth.

Success Journal Example

Skill: Un-Ableness Question	
What are you (we) unable to do, that if you (we) could do it, would solve the problem?	
7 X in 21 Days	**Successes and Results**
Date 1: *Sept 1*	*Asked Bill when he complained about test group*
Date 2: *Sept 5*	*Refocused team after re-org announcement*
Date 3:	
Date 4: *Sept 7*	*Ask boss for additional resources. Use we version*
Date 5:	
Date 6:	
Date 7:	

Use the Concepts

Apply the concepts explained in this handbook:

- Focus on a skill and making a commitment to develop that specific skill.

- Practice the particular skills at least 7 times in 21 days to internalize them.

- Document your successes, partial successes, and good intentions to increase your retention.

To start, pick one or two skills. Keep track of when you used them (or when you realized you should have used them) during the 21-day period. Record the date and comment on the results in your Success Journal, then move on to other skills.

Plan the Practice

Look at your calendar for the next 21 days and select opportunities to apply a particular skill. You might have a team meeting or a meeting with customers coming up. Outside of work, it may be a committee you're on or a social event. Log the dates on your calendar and the skill you'll practice, then record the results afterward in your Success Journal.

Review Often

Review your interactions at the end of the day or the end of each week and log the situations that were instructive. Identify situations in which you could have used a particular skill. Remember those situations in which you did use a skill by recording the date and success. Note: It's not critical that you have planned it.

Once you've mastered one or two skills, you can move on to others. All the while, you will be accruing the benefits of better interpersonal interactions.

Your reward is getting through life with more successes and results while experiencing fewer hassles and frustrations.

Who do I interact with to master the concepts?

Share the skills from this handbook with others: co-workers, your team, family, friends, and social groups. Teaching others is an action that has double benefits.

First, you learn more as you prepare and teach a skill to someone else.

Second, the people you teach can use these skills too. That way, all of your interactions will be more effective with fewer hassles.

Imagine if all of the people you interact with applied these skills.

- Whining, moaning, and groaning would be significantly reduced.

- People would provide the information in a way that the other person preferred.

- Behavior Requests would be direct and effective.

- Conflict would be significantly reduced.

- Everyone would get a lot more positive feedback.

It truly would be great to be part of this group.

Make a Behavior Contract

How do I stay committed?

Make a behavior contract with yourself. Write down the behaviors you are willing to commit to. Print it out. Sign it. Post it as your reminder to continue to grow and develop your skills. For example:

I agree to implement these behaviors:

★I will honor others' SOCIAL STYLE and change both my verbal and nonverbal communication to adapt to their style.

★I will use the Un-Ableness Question in individual conversations and group meetings to help move the Problem-Solving Process forward.

★To build trust, I will deliver the Core Dimensions of Respect, Empathy, Specificity, and Genuineness in every interaction.

★I will ask Two-Frame-of-Reference questions when I need information, and I will use the Behavior Request format when I need action.

★I will use the appropriate Behavior Request format to confront others and ask for what I need.

★If someone's behavior is causing me a problem, I will think through the steps of the Confrontation Checklist and either confront or let it go within 48 hours.

★I will give a clear "no" at the moment, accompanied by a valid business reason. I will remain open to negotiation and re-prioritization.

134

★When making a Behavior Request of another, I will avoid tangents by re-focusing the discussion and using No Strategies.

★I will accept "no" if the other person is willing to accept the consequences.

★I will give positive feedback at least once a week. If I don't get it, I will use confrontation to ask for it.

_____

(Signature)

Dick Cochran is a People Skills Expert that develops higher performing teams by creating more effective individuals.

In 1994 Dick brought together his twenty-five years of business experience in the Electronic Test & Measurement Industry with the "people skills" he learned in real team applications. He founded COMStar; a Training Company that helps teams and individuals on a world-wide basis become more effective.

The skills in his book *It Needs To Be Done: How to get others to do it with less hassle and stress;* have been thoroughly tested over the years through Dick's work with individual businesses and organizations. His People Skills training programs have created a positive cultural shift for both Government and non-Government clients.

This book presents the Dynamic Influencing Model© and is a handbook of the six tried and true skills needed to be successful in the team environment, either as a team member or team leader.

In 1997 Dick joined the Denver Mile Hi chapter of PMI (The Project Management Institute) and has been actively engaged in bringing his People Skills to Project Management Professionals.

Another great benefit of "People Skills" is that you can use them outside of work as well. Wouldn't it be great to improve your interactions outside of work, with your friends, the committees you are on, your church groups, and even with your family.

Dick and his wife Mary Ann live in Westminster, Colorado. Dick is an avid walker of their Airedale terrier named Panache. Panache keeps Dick and himself physically fit and the local rabbit population in a state of harassment.

To learn more about how to improve your interactions with others go to www.comstar.us

www.ingramcontent.com/pod-product-compliance
Lightning Source LLC
Chambersburg PA
CBHW031944190326
41519CB00007B/650

* 9 7 8 0 9 9 9 6 5 0 8 6 0 5 *